A WORLD WITHOUT HUNGER

by
J. Harry Haines

Other books by the author:

Christianity and Communism
The Chinese of the Diaspora
The Twain Shall Meet

Library of Congress
Copyright

Contents

This book is dedicated to the many committed people who have given of themselves in Christian service through Church World Service in every part of the world. And we especially remember colleagues who gave their lives while working with Vietnam Christian Service.

Daniel Gerber (Mennonite Central Committee), reported missing May 30, 1962.

Gloria Redlin (Lutheran World Relief), killed by gunfire October 21, 1970.

Ted Studebaker (Church World Service), killed by gunfire April 26, 1971.

PREFACE

We are living in a time when many American Christians are concerned and depressed about the church. Membership is smaller, money harder to get, youth work seems less effective, the ecumenical enthusiasm of the recent past seems to be waning. What a joy—then—to discover a book which details dramatically the story of our churches, working together, bringing life and hope to God's children in need all around the world!

I thought I knew all about Church World Service, but I quickly found myself caught up by this story with a growing sense of wonder and amazement. Because it is *our* story, the story of ordinary American Christian men and women and youth, who have been practicing cooperation in the relief of human suffering, and in bringing new life and freedom to millions of our fellow human beings. From an earthquake in Guatemala, starvation in Africa and Asia, conflict and tragedy in the Middle East and Ireland, the plight of millions of refugees, and the urgent needs for development and human rights, this tale of Christian caring lifts our sights, and our spirits.

It is not written that way. In fact, it is largely just a straightforward account of what was done and why it was done that way. Not every episode is a success story, but we learned from our failures. It tells dramatic tales of emergency help, but balances these with accounts of careful, undramatic plans and efforts to help people develop their own abilities to meet their own needs. It has no need to preach ecumenism because it is so abundantly clear that no single church could ever have met the needs, and that uncoordinated separate efforts would have been disastrous.

While Church World Service is an agency of those churches which make up the National Council of Churches, the cooperation described here goes far beyond that—often including Roman Catholics, Southern Baptists, evangelical groups, secular agencies and governments. Begun largely to provide emergency relief in time of disaster, CWS soon realized that helping people develop their own skills to meet their own needs was a much more important task.

One cannot read this story without a deep feeling of thankfulness that we have been privileged to be a part of such a glorious chapter in the history of the churches. It is, in one sense, a worthy sequel to the great missionary movement of the late nineteenth and early twentieth century. Nor does it stop there. The last chapters raise real questions about what we—as American Christians—should be doing in the years ahead. The world is changing, ever more rapidly. We all need to become involved in the dialogue about the mission of the Church in this changing world. This book can be a catalyst for such a dialogue—in a local church, a denomination, councils of churches—wherever "two or three are gathered together in His Name."

Cynthia C. Wedel

Past President, National Council of the
Churches of Christ in the U.S.A.
President, World Council of Churches

INTRODUCTION

Just as the manuscript of this book was being completed, the Presidential Commission on World Hunger released its preliminary report. Much of the analysis and the reasons for the fact that hundreds of millions of people go to bed hungry every night of their lives covers familiar ground but the conclusion of the document does propose a challenge to the United States, to the affluent West, and in turn has suggested the title for this book, *A World Without Hunger.* The Presidential Commission says that if the United States could bring to bear on this great problem the same determination and technology that it has brought to other problems, that hunger indeed could be banished from the earth by the end of this century; that there is no reason for multitudes of people to live out their lives in quiet despair with the only issue for them being one of survival.

A similar conclusion was reached some years ago at the Rome Conference on World Hunger called by the United Nations when some 120 nations gathered for 2½ weeks in that city with one single agenda item—to do something about World Hunger. At that time the conclusions were similar except the Secretary General of the conference said: "We know how to banish hunger and it can be done in one generation, but we do not know how to change people and systems to make it possible." Perhaps this is what it really is all about, or as the new popular cliche has come into usage: "This is really the bottom line."

In 1965 Harold Fey, for many years editor of the Christian Century, wrote a history of Church World Service covering its beginning years. There has been expressed many times recently desire for a history of

Church World Service, the ecumenical agency that has brought together 31 Protestant denominations within the National Council of Churches, to bring that history up to date. This book is an effort to do this. It has a very different kind of structure than the earlier history and because of the vastness of the enterprise, the great numbers of people involved, it has proved utterly impossible to cover the whole operation. Therefore, there have been chosen ten representative areas of the world.

Lacking the resources of the United Nations or intergovernmental agencies, the story in fact is a very modest one. But it is a story of determination by a number of men and women who are not prepared to accept things the way they are, who believe that the proof of their faith is in their caring and in their sharing. A great many people have been and are today involved in this enterprise of doing something about the agony of the world.

This morning as I was writing this page, there came into my office an old friend who himself twenty years ago was involved with Church World Service in resettling refugees. Today he and his wife live in Greece in retirement, but on a very brief stay in New York he wanted to come by and leave a substantial personal check to say: "I want CWS to know that I care; I have been involved; and I want to see the American churches going on being involved in reaching out to people in the name of Christ saying we care about you and we want to help." This is perhaps the spirit of this organization.

If I were to dedicate this book, I would dedicate it to the hundreds of volunteers, of staff who over the years and who today are scattered across five continents, to one lonely representative who sits in an office in Phnom Penh, Kampuchea, battling with the maddening difficulties of working with government officials who have on their hands something which has been likened to the second Holocaust. He is there on our behalf trying to get food and medical supplies out to the people who need it. He does not consider himself a hero. He is just doing a job that has to be done and for this we are profoundly grateful. I want to recognize the previous directors of CWS, some of them in retirement, others occupied with other tasks today, but who are a part of the unique fellowship that for me personally began when in 1952 I became the first Church World Service field representative in Southeast Asia, until today in the closing hours of 1979. As I look out my office window at 475 Riverside Drive and realize that around the world in hundreds of communities this unique bringing together of people of many different denominational loyalties into a single task to feed the hungry, to clothe

the naked, to release the prisoner, is amazing. I have often been asked the question: How successful is Church World Service in its global operation? My answer is always the same. It is as successful as the congregations of Christ's people across our lands want it to be in that they make available the resources to see that human need is met.

Success stories? Yes, there are lots of them. Many books could be filled with them. Failure? Yes, there have been failures and disappointments that have occasioned tears at times. But, above all, the original commitment of Church World Service prevails. It is an agency brought into being by the churches of America, member churches of the National Council of Churches, who discovered that the things that united them were far more important than those that divided them and were determined to do this part of their task together. This is really what it is all about.

There are many people who should be identified as having made a particular and special contribution to this book. Above all, I want to thank the present Executive Director, Dr. Paul McCleary, veteran Latin American missionary, church mission board executive, and today the one who carries the major responsibility of directing this agency, and to Dr. Tracey Early who assisted in much of the background research and editing that brought all this story together. Perhaps a very special word needs to be said, not only of our American staff, but of the countless numbers of colleagues in some 70 countries who have put their lives on the line and who really helped to make it all possible for Christ's sake.

Some day the entire story of Church World Service will be told and recorded. In the meantime, this book is offered as a bringing together of the tumultuous years between 1965 and New Year's Day 1980.

J. Harry Haines
Hemlock Farms
Lent, 1980

The Churches Together in Service to the World

Recently an enterprising reporter in New York City decided to write a feature article listing the tragic events that had occurred in the previous 24 hours in that city. He listed the number of robberies, bank hold ups, muggings, murders, homocide cases, and when he had completed this unhappy listing, he concluded with these words: "Of all these events, we were unwilling witnesses." As I read this article, the words, "of all these events, we were unwilling witnesses," seemed to leap off the page. Throughout the day, they simply would not let go of me. I just kept thinking about all these unwilling witnesses and these terrifying events. When we turn to recounting the events that have surrounded the last fifteen year history of Church World Service, many of these are events of great tragedy and sorrow, impacting hundreds of thousands, if not millions of lives. Yet of these we are not so much unwilling witnesses, as we would record the experiences of people who not only have been caught up in the tragedy of life around them, but of those who have reached out and said in the name of God: "We care about you." This book is really all about caring, caring for people and while there will have to be dates recorded, institutions and organizations involved, I really would like to take you with me on a journey around the world to see the church in action reaching out to people saying and proving that we really do care about them.

The question is often asked: What is God doing in our world? Sometimes the question is put another way: What in earth is the church doing in the world about human need? So we have to begin perhaps with refugees, the hallmark of humankind's inhumanity to other human beings. This century has been rightfully called the century of the homeless person. Later on in this book we will be talking in detail about these refugees and what is being done. When refugees began streaming out of Vietnam, Laos and Kampuchea (Cambodia), U.S. Christians wanted to help them find new homes. Through Church World Service, the Protestant and Orthodox Churches, assisted tens of thousands of Indochinese coming to the United States and helped them to rebuild their lives again, as they had done through the years for refugees from Cuba, Haiti, Hungary, Iraq, Uganda and many, many other countries. When the news of a second Holocaust broke upon the world press, reporting that over 3,000,000 people had perished from starvation or disease in Kampuchea, there was an agency that could and did move immediately into action. It launched immediately an emergency appeal for $5,000,000 and member churches within a few weeks met that appeal in full. Staff were sent for an on the spot investigation and an office was opened in Phnom Penh to work in close cooperation with other relief agencies and the United Nations, who oversee the distribution of aid. All this was done because this is the nature of the church, to reach out and touch people's lives with the help they so desperately need.

Hurricane David brought destruction to the Caribbean in the summer 1979. Tens of thousands of people lost their homes and possessions. It was not necessary to call a conference to study the matter, design ways to help. They already had preparations made because on an average of once every eight days somewhere around the world disaster strikes people and help must be sent immediately. One of the things the U.S. Protestant and Orthodox churches have discovered in this arm of compassion is that no one of them by themselves has sufficient resources to respond to these devastating needs. Someone rightly said that if Church World Service was disbanded today by tomorrow morning representatives of the churches would have to meet and create another agency immediately. For such is the nature of the world in which we live that only through cooperative action can help be mobilized on such a scale that it really helps to make a difference.

Around the world in 70 countries U.S. churches through Church World Service join hands with similar agencies in Western Europe, Great Britain, Australia, New Zealand, and in many parts of the Third World to bring the kind of help that is needed in the hour of great need. The final goal of all of this cannot be relief. Relief is essential for those first days following a disaster, when blankets, food, medicine and trained personnel are moved quickly into the area, but beyond relief

2

there has to be the rebuilding of the lives of people, the reconstruction of their society. There will be many references in this book to Church World Service, but the purpose is not to simply glorify the agency, or to point out how great it is, but to say it is the channel or the catalyst whereby Christians may join their arms and their hands together. It is really Christians acting together.

Because of the long experience in dealing with disaster needs, it was found necessary many years ago to have a central stockpile where millions of dollars worth of clothing, blankets, medical supplies, hospital equipment could be held ready for an emergency call. When news broke on the world press that 500,000 Afghans had poured across the frontier seeking asylum in Pakistan in January 1980, the kind of help that was needed had to move immediately. For the staff in New Windsor, Maryland, where there is a $5,000,000 stockpile, it was not an extraordinary situation to be told to load trucks with 30,000 blankets and five tons of clothing and medicine and leave immediately for Baltimore-Washington International Airport where a chartered DC 8 cargo jet was waiting to load 45 tons of supplies on board and 17 hours later unloaded in Islamabad, Pakistan, where trucks were waiting with a field representative of CWS to escort the trucks to the camps.

By 1977 it had become apparent to all the churches that a domestic disaster office was needed to deal with the many emergencies that occur here in the United States. In the next eight months it was to give assistance in more than fifty emergency situations. The director of the domestic operation, with over thirty years experience in handling disasters, is able to give not only supplies to supplement what the Red Cross or other relief agencies can supply, but a different role is very often filled. After a disaster, people commonly suffer from shock. They need someone to help mobilize them in the work of rebuilding. Specialists may be brought in to help pastors deal with the counseling needs of people who have lost family members, homes and personal possessions. In other ways, local churches gain reinforcement in the performance of their ministry.

The churches then, are organized for cooperative action at home or abroad. Christians in the U.S. respond to needs even before they have given their offerings, perhaps before many of them have heard that the need exists. When they see the headlines reporting a new disaster, they can know with certainty that behind the headlines the churches are already at work, moving into action even before receiving funds to finance the action. The churches operate on the proven belief that when Christians learn of human suffering anywhere in the world, they will respond.

In spiritual terms CWS is the response to the words of Jesus, "As you did it to one of the least of these my brethren, you did it to me." (Matthew 25:40) These "least" members of the human family who suffer from most acute and immediate need have first call on the compassion of Christians.

This statement by Jesus is not a marginal emphasis of the Bible, but part of the central theme. Jesus was reiterating the teaching of the Torah, "You shall open wide your hand to your brother, to the needy and to the poor . . ." (Deut. 15:11)

And he was continuing in the tradition of the prophets:

Is not this the fast that I choose:
  to loose the bonds of wickedness,
  to undo the thongs of the yoke,
  to let the oppressed go free,
  and to break every yoke?
Is it not to share your bread with the hungry,
  and bring the homeless poor into your house;
When you see the naked, to cover him,
  and not to hide yourself from your own flesh?
                        (Isaiah 58:6-7)

The Psalmist wrote that the Lord provides "justice for the needy" (Ps. 140:12), and proverbial wisdom taught that "he who is kind to the poor lends to the Lord, and he will repay him for his deed." (Prov. 19:18)

Jesus reinforced this tradition and made it a living reality in the new community of his disciples. At a time of distress for the early church, those Christians who had possessions sold them and shared so that "there was not a needy person among them." (Acts 4:34) Later the Apostle Paul collected money to assist the Jerusalem church. "I do not mean that others should be eased and you burdened," he wrote, "but that as a matter of equality your abundance at the present time should supply their want." (2 Cor. 8:13-14).

The churches assist people in need without regard to their race, nationality, or political ideology, and also without regard to their religion. But they feel a special obligation to assist Christians in need. And in parts of the world where Christians form a small minority, the social situation often becomes oppressive and creates a need for the international Christian community to show its solidarity. Christians who may be pushed to the side in their own region can gain increased

4

confidence as they realize that they form part of a worldwide church, and that this body feels the suffering endured by its members anywhere in the world.

Dr. John Mackay, Presbyterian theologian and for many years the distinguished President of Princeton Theological Seminary in Princeton, New Jersey, on a number of occasions said to us as his students, "There are two great symbols of the Christian faith, the cross which is so important a part of our life, it reminds us of the life, death and resurrection of our Lord. But there is another symbol of the Christian faith, which is seldom spoken of. That is the symbol of the basin of water and the towel, evidence of the servanthood of the Church." Perhaps it is this theological symbol, the basin and towel, that has become so important in the life of this cooperative agency.

Historically, CWS is the product of several strands of church efforts to cooperate in the service of human need which date back to the early part of this century when an earthquake and drought created famine in 1920-21 in China. Missionaries, Chinese Christians and the Chinese business community formed a China International Famine Relief Committee, which at one time was feeding 8,000,000 people. This Committee used a technique that was to become standard in later church relief work—food for work. Those of able body were sent to work on useful projects: 850 miles of roads, irrigation of 15,000 acres of land, some 3,600 wells. Food was given as wages. Instead of becoming dependent on a dole, left in idleness, people retained their dignity as they earned their food. They could see their work contributing to the development of their country. Taking a long range view the Committee later gave its unused funds to Nanking College of Agriculture and Yenching University in Peking for work on measures to prevent future famines.

As a United States counterpart to the Committee on China, the Federal Council of Churches and the Foreign Missions Conference organized China Famine Relief. Other agencies were created from time to time, all of them brought into being by the overwhelming sense of need which could only be met as hands and hearts were joined together in a magnificent outpouring of compassion. After World War II the U.S. churches decided they had to have one single agency that could move rapidly anywhere in the world on a continuing basis to not only bring relief, but also the reconstruction of peoples' homes and their lives. The mystique of Church World Service, if it has one, is that it really represents the bringing together of the denominational agencies that have almost identical mandates. And so it looks to its

5

member churches for them to interpret to their communions what the world situation is, what the needs are. From each member denomination funds are provided for this ecumenical action; personnel are recruited, so that this dimension of the churches' life and witness is joined with the mission outreach of the churches, which for over 150 years had been involved in evangelization and missionary outreach. These two arms of the churches' life, often referred to as "mission" and "service," or, in the World Council of Churches, they were spoken of as "Life and Work," and "Faith and Order," began in 1950 as two separate arms of the National Council of Churches. But in 1965 the two were brought together in the newly created Division of Overseas Ministries (DOM). There have been times when these two aspects of the churches' witness, mission and service, have been sharply distinguished, but in recent years the churches have increasingly recognized that service is an intrinsic part of mission.

Such a perspective reflects the actual experience of missionaries who have given relief as a normal part of their work, and it reflects the Christian understanding of service, that refuses to separate concern for body and soul. It feeds the hungry, but also shows concern for the human dignity of those who are served and helps them become more deeply aware of their place in the family of God. CWS staff serve as Division staff. Within the Division of Overseas Ministries are the units: Agricultural Missions, Intermedia, Associated Mission Medical Office, Overseas Personnel, Leadership Development, Human Rights, and International Congregations and Lay Ministries. These are the units which together seek to be effective tools in the hands of God.

There are many questions asked by people of Church World Service. How do you decide where to help and whom to help? Is CWS for Christians only? Does it only work in countries where there are governments friendly to ours? Who decides anyhow what it should do? There is one criterion that dominates the scene. Simply stated, it is human need. The need for response on behalf of those who follow in the steps of the one who fed the hungry, the confused, and the weary by the shores of a lake in Israel long ago.

When it became possible to begin work on behalf of starving Kampucheans, the churches faced the question of which Kampucheans to help, which channels they would use. Most Kampucheans by 1979 were living under the Phnom Penh government of Heng Samrin, which seemed more humane than its predecessor, but owed most of its power to the Vietnamese who had come in to help them. Other

6

Kampucheans still followed the former rule of Pol Pot, who had led a government virtually unprecedented in the twentieth century for savagery and cruelty against its own people. Still others formed parts of various resistance groups, or languished in refugee camps in Thailand. Helping one group would make the leaders of the other groups suspicious. And if the churches decided to help Kampucheans outside the country as well as those remaining inside, they still faced the question of how much emphasis to place on each.

The DOM executive director, Eugene Stockwell, told the CWS Committee as it faced this issue: "We are inevitably involved in ambiguities. We cannot be purely humanitarian and I doubt that we can achieve equity to all parties. We will face difficult and imperfect choices."

Still, the choice and the decision had to be made. They were to turn to member churches across the nation, alert them to the fact that we were confronted with one of the greatest disasters of the twentieth century compared by many to the Holocaust of World War II. Wherever there were Kampucheans who could be reached, whether in Phnom Penh or on the border of Thailand; wherever help could be sent, it would be sent in Christ's name.

Perhaps we need at this point to explain a little clearer just exactly how the churches work together, what kind of network is there, and without going into too many complex details, we have to begin with the fact that the churches of the United States are not alone in this task. We really are a part of a world church, and that through regional councils in Africa, Asia, Latin America, the Middle East and the Pacific, we link up in a great partnership of faith and compassion. In 70 countries around the world we are able to help churches in these countries to carry out the mandate of their Lord and Master to care and feed the hungry and to bind up the wounds of those who in the long march of humanity towards a new and better day are left wounded by the side of the road.

And so it is not surprising to find that in so many of these countries you will not find American representatives. You will find representatives of the churches there administering to their people, reinforced with international assistance, which may bring together food and funds from many parts of the world. Much of Church World Service's work is made possible by its relationship to the World Council of Churches which now includes some 300 different member churches.

When a tidal wave and cyclone hit India in 1977 with the loss of 85,000 lives, assistance was given through the Indian Churches

Auxiliary for Social Action (CASA). Rather than go into a country and launch a program of its own, CWS prefers to work with an agency of the country's own churches which takes the lead, and gives support to what it undertakes.

This approach strengthens local churches and helps them become more effective in service to their own societies. And it encourages them to operate ecumenically. Often CWS serves as a catalyst in drawing together churches that have not previously cooperated with each other. In this way mission churches can sometimes develop closer patterns of cooperation with each other than their parent churches in the United States and Europe have achieved.

Though CWS as a Protestant and Orthodox agency normally looks first to agencies of Protestant and Orthodox churches abroad, it sometimes works through Roman Catholic or other agencies not directly related to its members. And though it looks first to the churches to find its "colleague agencies," it does not totally confine itself to these circles. Judging according to particular circumstances, sometimes it seems best to work through government or private agencies.

This international network has helped in a special way where resentment of U.S. political and economic power has made people suspicious of aid from U.S. churches. In such situations willingness to offer aid as part of some larger international program, joining with agencies such as Christian Aid Great Britain, German Evangelische Hilfswerk and Brot für die Welt, French CIMADE, and others often makes North American aid more acceptable.

Years of work through the international network have produced not only patterns of cooperation with colleague agencies, but also personal ties between American staff and individuals in these agencies. CWS considers relationships of mutual trust and understanding as one of the strongest assets of the agency. And it has come through an emphasis on people-to-people contact.

The network of various relief and development agencies in the United States includes CODEL, a New York based agency formed in 1969 by Protestant and Catholic mission societies working in development; TECHNOSERV, an agency organized to provide technical, managerial and financial assistance to locally owned enterprises to train participants; Partnership for Productivity, concerned with rural development in Africa; PACT (Private Agencies Collaborating Together); International Voluntary Services, that challenges skilled volunteers to help the rural poor in the Third World develop self reliance; and The Heifer Project which assists poor farmers with better technical and management skills. These are but a few of what many of us call our ecumenical partners, or satellite agencies, all concerned with finding resources and bringing them to bear on the needs of people.

Another question frequently asked is, How is Church World Service funded? Much of the money that denominations channel to CWS and our other relief and development agencies is raised by the interdenominational appeal, the One Great Hour of Sharing, which is usually taken during the Lenten period of the churches calendar. It brings many millions of dollars into cooperative service.

Perhaps the best known part of CWS to local churches, especially in the rural areas of the United States is CROP, organized as the Christian Rural Overseas Program. In 1947 American Christians, particularly farmers in the Midwest, contributed grain and other commodities for shipment to needy people abroad. By 1952 it had become an integral part of CWS primarily for raising funds through community events. In 1978 it expanded its attention to consciousness raising and hunger education. Reflecting this change, this part of CWS is now known as the Constituency Education and Fundraising Unit. The CROP name is used to identify fundraising activities.

Many challenging ways have been found by CROP to involve people across the country in campaigns such as hunger walkathons, miss a meal a week, haystack rides, bicycle rides, handicraft auctions. The various ways of fund raising are as numerous as the ingenuity of concerned men, women and young people. The main purpose has been to get people involved in the fight against hunger. Since the mandate of the Constituency Education and Fundraising Unit is hunger education as well as fundraising, it seeks to educate through the ways that it raises funds.

All these are part of the total impact of people reaching out to other people. The United States government has recognized the important role of this agency and annually provides a substantial part of the CWS expenses in freight reimbursement and provision of food under Public Law 480.

"There is a lad here who has five barley loaves and two fish; but what are they among so many?" asked the Apostle Andrew in John 6:9. A hungry multitude stood before Jesus and the resources seemed ridiculously meager. Jesus took the gift, gave thanks for it and used it to meet the need.

Though from some perspectives the 40 million dollar annual

9

program of Church World Service may seem large, in relation to a world of 4 billion people with half a billion or more in acute need, it seems ridiculously small. But like the boy who gave his loaves and fish to Jesus, the churches offer what they have with faith that the Lord will multiply the value of whatever is placed in His hands.

CWS sees its contributions multiplied in many ways, often it finances a pioneering project that is later taken up on a broader scale by United Nations agencies, national governments or other bodies with greater resources. Sometimes a small contribution serves as an endorsement of a project and consequently brings aid from other agencies that trust CWS judgment. CWS is too small to act in human pride, but it has found that it can act in faith.

Factors of special importance for the success of this program over the years include:

—flexibility: the ability to respond to all types of disasters, at home and abroad, and to such diverse needs as chronic poverty, tensions in Ulster and resettlement of refugees;

—visibility: the ability of people to see that the churches are responding, moving into action where need is greatest;

—integrity: the determination to report honestly on what has been accomplished, and what has not been accomplished, avoiding inflated reports that might temporarily offer "inspiration" but in the end reduce confidence and respect;

—ecumenicity: the conviction that the churches should work cooperatively rather than in isolation or in competition, and that they should encourage movements for cooperative work in other countries.

2

Guatemala—How Long Will You Stay?

Early in the morning before dawn on February 4, 1976, Guatemala was hit by the worst earthquake in the recorded history of Central America. On the Richter scale it registered 7.5, almost as severe as the historic San Francisco earthquake of 1906.

The Guatemala earthquake killed 25,000 people and injured 70,000 more. It left a million people homeless, out of a total population of six million—a percentage equivalent to more than 35 million in the United States.

CWS learned of the disaster within five hours from a ham radio operator who got a message from Mrs. Joan Parajon in Managua, Nicaragua. Its first action was to ask church agencies in Nicaragua and Honduras to send in relief supplies, with CWS reimbursing part of the cost.

Within hours relief supplies were entering by plane. By the time many U.S. church members were learning about the disaster from morning news broadcasts, their agency had food, medicine, clothing and blankets on the way. Later, shiploads of aid arrived.

But after the immediate crisis had passed and the world turned its attention to other matters, CWS began rehabilitation programs to help the people rebuild their homes and communities. And from that it moved into more long range programs of development and helping Guatemalans deal with the fundamental causes of their poverty.

The effort in Guatemala was strengthened by an earlier experience in Nicaragua. CWS became involved in Central America for the first time when an earthquake hit Managua in 1972. This led to the establishment of a cooperative church agency, CEPAD (Evangelical

11

Committee for Disaster Response), later reorganized as Evangelical Committee for Development. U.S. churches relied on CEPAD, and a neighbor agency in Honduras, CEDEN (Evangelical Committee for Development and National Emergencies), to provide initial help in Guatemala.

When the civil war tore at Nicaragua in 1978-79, preceding the ouster of President Anastasio Somoza, CEPAD staff were seasoned veterans meeting the needs of the people whose lives were wracked by war. CEPAD served as the distributor of 800 tons of corn, beans, rice, powdered milk and other food sent by CWS and coordinated relief throughout the country through a network of regional and local committees.

In an especially clear way, the three part program of assistance in Guatemala illustrates the CWS approach. Immediate needs are not neglected in the interest of pursuing long range goals. When disaster strikes, people must have help at once. They require food and medicine and other basics. And in the confusion and bewilderment of sudden tragedy, they need the assurance that they are not alone in the world. Christians in Guatemala were immediately reminded that they belonged to a global community that responded to the pain of any member.

But neither do the churches consider it sufficient to meet the immediate needs. Many compassionate people will offer help right after a disaster occurs, but then quickly go on to other things. The church so easily becomes prone to "compassion fatigue."

CWS recognizes that people who have been hit by an earthquake or flood or famine will continue to need help over an extended period, as they spend months putting their lives together again.

Pressing still deeper, it recognizes that enduring problems of poverty and social injustice have made many people more vulnerable to natural disaster than they ought to be. Their housing is often flimsy and too easily demolished. Their living standards are marginal with no reserves for emergencies. Their political power and ability to influence public bodies are too limited to command an effective reaction to their needs. A disaster uncovers the more fundamental, long term problems so the churches go on to help people come to grips with these dimensions of their plight.

Three days after the earthquake a team of three of us arrived in Guatemala City. There were still hundreds of small tremors as the aftermath of the earthquake, and most of the buildings, in the capital city were considered unsafe. Half of the hotel we checked into was so

12

On February 4, 1976, Guatamala suffered the most severe earthquake ever recorded in Central America. Within hours CWS had received a report relayed via ham radio and set in motion a response which was to become one of the largest ever begun by the agency.
(CWS photo)

badly damaged it ultimately had to be torn down and rebuilt.

As we gathered with heads of major Protestant churches and mission groups that afternoon, the first amazing thing we discovered was that most of them simply did not know each other. Various groups had lived largely in isolation from each other. What decades of traditional missionary work had not been able to do, this terrifying disaster had succeeded in doing—bringing them together so that they could look at their tasks.

The first question that was asked was, "how long are you going to stay?" The vast majority of the international and overseas agencies had arrived in Guatemala and within a very short time would leave again. The construction phase, however, would prove to be the most difficult and, at the same time the most necessary. My reply on behalf of the U.S. churches was that we would stay three years. But it was important that the assistance being provided not become a crutch, but be designed to help people get on their feet again. Perhaps the greatest gift that we have to give to people is the gift of dignity, to reach out with a caring hand and help them to stand up on their feet and to rebuild their shattered lives, and they in turn to reach out to others.

Sometime later as it was decided to make a filmstrip that told the story of the CWS involvement in Guatemala, we told this story around the life of a young Indian woman, Esperanza Chacon, in the village of Nueva Chinautla. The woman, whose name means hope, was a young artist who made ceramic doves. Most of the people in her village are artisans—weavers, potters or artists. All of them found that their homes and their equipment lay in ruins. The shattered fragments of one of Esperanza's shattered doves became the focal point for the recounting of what had happened in Guatemala. In a sense her own personal story is the story of her people. "La Paloma de Esperanza," (The Dove of Hope), begins with a shattered dove in the studio. The shattered fragments could never, never again be put back together. The solution was to take new clay and to create a new dove. We follow Esperanza as she goes to the outskirts of her shattered village, seeking to find the right clay. Then we watch her take this clay and with skillful hands fashion it into a beautiful new dove, symbolizing peace and symbolizing for her people a resurrection.

This was the great problem that faced Guatemala. A million people lost their homes. How could they be helped with dignity to rebuild their homes and lives? The commitment which had begun with planeloads of food and blankets and clothing within a very short time had to be stopped. The major task of helping them rebuild their homes became critical. This could be done in one of two ways. We could bring in the latest techniques of housing construction and rebuild their homes for them. Perhaps in the doing of it there would be unconsciously a paternalistic attitude toward them, or we could help them and their neighbors get together in groups and rebuild their own homes so they could say at the end, "this is our house, we built it."

With so many people homeless the immediate priority was roofing, especially as the rainy season was approaching. Zinc coated steel roofing was imported from the United States and distributed through various church and community groups. Then lumber was imported and cemented steel bars were brought from Honduras and Mexico. These materials helped in the reconstruction of 17,000 homes, and the construction later of thousands in other locations, CWS agreed to provide $500,000, later increased to $600,000 in cash and material to CEMEC. This was an agency of the local church that was building new houses in a suburb of Guatemala City for the landless, urban poor. Norwegian Church Aid contributed another $500,000. In Carolingia, 10,000 people moved in and began putting together their *champas* (shacks) out of scraps of wood, plastic, cardboard, whatever they could find. The government then invited CEMEC to build a "model of human settlement" of 1500 houses and other community buildings. Each family was to contribute fifteen days of labor or the cash equivalent, and pay $10 per month for a house and lot. With variations such arrangements were made for other housing projects in which the churches became involved.

In late 1976 and early 1977 CWS took on other housing construction projects where it provided all the funding—in Nueva Chinautla, Joyita de San Antonio, Mixco and San Juan de Dios.

Construction was mostly cement block walls with steel roofing and cement floors. An exception was Mixco, where the "stack sack" construction was used. This involves filling sacks with a mixture of sand and cement and putting them in water to harden. They are then stacked to make walls, with iron rods connecting them together and a concrete spray skin is put on the outside. The result is a house notably non-traditional in appearance but unusually resistant to earthquakes.

Land for the housing projects came from the government housing bank, BANVI, which handled legal matters such as property deeds, and set up financial arrangements for house owners to pay for their lots over a 10-15 year period. Funds from sale of the houses were to be used for community centers, health centers and schools. CEMEC employed some social workers to help build a sense of community among new

15

neighbors.

Many volunteer workers came from the United States to help. Immediately after the earthquake medical teams offered service and a new sense of partnership was developed between these teams and the Guatemalan people, who really were quite overwhelmed by this kind of cooperative effort.

In many cases Guatemalans who would get the houses were contributing labor as part of the purchase price. Those who had other jobs sometimes hired substitutes. The people of Joyita decided that each family would contribute three *quetzals* (dollars) a week toward the workers' payroll. In addition, each family would make payments of ten quetzals a month for an averge of ten years for their house and lot. In return, they got an attractive three room house with bath— something below the standards of U.S. suburbanites—but far better than the housing they rented before the earthquake—and far better than the *champas* that had been their homes before the earthquake.

At the end of three years, as had been originally planned, the housing program was completed and by the end of the year CWS began to conclude its service to the people of the country. Work would go on with a new Guatemalan agency directed entirely by Guatemalan people. This would continue to deal with the root causes of hunger and oppression that had been revealed as a result of the earthquake.

CWS had planned its program for Guatemala like a military operation. At the beginning it determined in full consultation with its Guatemalan partners the overall strategy for the whole campaign.

—it would commit itself to stay for three years.
—it would mobilize the churches to act as the cutting edge.
—it would terminate the relief aspects of the operation in ninety days.
—it would begin major reconstruction in selected areas.
—it would stay long enough to work with fundamental needs, moving in its final phase into development.

North American churches provided $4,000,000 for this operation of assistance and reconstruction. At the end of three years, 20,000 Guatemalans had secured new homes.

There were many important lessons learned from the Guatemalan relief and reconstruction efforts. There was soon awareness of a need to screen and to orient volunteers who had willingly offered their service, most of them at their own expense, to spend several weeks in Guatemala. One nurse on duty at the time in a hospital in Pontiac,

16

Following the emergency relief phase in Guatamala, CWS operations turned to housing reconstruction. Houses were built of concrete blocks using steel sheeting for roofs and concrete slabs for floors.
(CWS photo)

Michigan, when told there was an urgent need for nurses, arranged with her supervisor at the conclusion of her shift at 6:00 p.m. to be given two months leave of absence. At 10:00 p.m. that night she was on a plane headed for Chicago with a connecting flight to Guatemala City. She had formerly worked in Latin America, spoke fluent Spanish, was oriented to the people, and her presence there was to be a great blessing to the people who she hoped to serve in the name of Christ. Other volunteers were not fluent in Spanish. They had had little experience outside their own home communities. Out of this experience ongoing training programs were started for volunteers who would respond to other disasters in the future.

The Guatemala experience also taught the wisdom of consulting local people about what is planned for them, or better still, to gather them to do the planning and implementing themselves. The urgent situation of a disaster creates a tendency for workers to rush in and keep rushing as they do their work.

After the relief efforts had concluded and the major housing program had come to a successful end, the third and the long term phase was to begin. Throughout the entire Third World one of the most tragic problems that effects the lives of hundreds of millions of people has been called the "land question," landless people who have no stake in their own future and the future of their children. There are many areas in Latin America and Central America where eighty percent of the arable land is owned or controlled by less than seven percent of the population. Guatemala is no exception. Absentee landlords control great areas of the highlands.

In the community of Kato-Ki an agricultural cooperative was established which bought *fincas* (large plantations) and broke them up into small units and sold them to groups of landless Guatemalan farmers who had been tenant farmers for endless generations. The cooperative lent them the purchase price at 12 percent interest—8 percent to cover administrative costs and 4 percent to build up the capital. The cooperatives also taught the farmers agricultural techniques, sold them seed and supplies at wholesale prices and marketed their crops for them. This organization, which had come into existence before the earthquake, was to now receive new impetus and bring hope where there had been no hope for so many people.

It is a tradition in the highlands of Guatemala for thousands of Indian farmers to go to the coast each year to work on the great plantations of cotton and other crops. They sell themselves into penury. Many who went before never returned. They left their homes and families in dire financial need. Now because of land cooperatives like Kato-Ki, many would never again have to make that lonely journey to the coast, but could work their own land.

Development work in Guatemala would also include projects in public health and nutrition. In the Central highlands the predominantly Indian population, descendents of the ancient Mayas, were treated by fifty health promoters who had been trained at the Behrhorst Clinic in Chimaltenango. Here again is an exciting story of how one man decided that the traditional method of running a modern, American style hospital in the community was really no answer at all to the needs of the people.

Carroll Behrhorst, recruited originally by the Missouri Synod Lutheran Church, had been sent to Chimaltenango to build a new hospital. Instead, he was to begin a revolutionary method of medicine by training Indian men and women as health promoters, known in more recent years as barefoot doctors because of the success of an almost identical program in the People's Republic of China. His men and women were each established as independent business people. They were trained at the hospital and then returned to their community. They were trained not only in modern medicine, but also in agriculture, so they became good farmers, as well as good public health doctors. Tens of thousands of Indians who had been denied even rudimentary medical care now for the first time in their lives were to get that help for themselves and for their children.

Land, water, good medical care, education, housing—these are the elements that we so often take for granted. Guatemala's tragic earthquake revealed not only its great needs, but gave to the churches in Guatemala their first opportunity to be part of the answer to the needs of their people. There will continue to be many Guatemalas in the years ahead, but the lessons learned there were to prove absolutely invaluable. The churches could come out of their isolation from one another and begin this task of responding to the needs of the people around them. Once again, the towel and the basin became the symbol of the church, along with the symbol of the cross.

3

Sahel—
Change or Perish

In one of the most isolated areas of the world, a precariously balanced ecology silently tipped over and took the lives of 100,000 people. But the crisis was underway for five years before the world knew it existed. The drought in the Sahel was, to most people, an invisible disaster.

The Sahel encompasses the area just below the Sahara Desert. According to the United Nations definition, it includes Mauritania, Upper Volta, Mali, Niger and Chad. For CWS it also includes Senegal and the northern parts of Guinea, Ghana, Benin, Togo and Nigeria. And the drought actually affected a belt running all across the continent and, in varying patterns, circling the globe.

This African area, stretching more than 2000 miles, was supporting a small population at a bare survival level. But when rainfall suddenly decreased in 1968, and continued at an extraordinarily low level year after year until 1974, large numbers of the people could no longer survive at all without help.

Many of them were nomads depending on cattle, which they drove in a generally south to north route over a cycle of years, moving from one oasis and grazing area to another, and trading with more sedentary tribes. When the drought came, a million head of cattle died and the limited crop production declined.

Once the extent of the disaster became generally known, governments, including the United States and other countries, created an international task force to bring relief. Roads in the area were primitive, where they existed at all, so aid was mostly delivered by air drop.

20

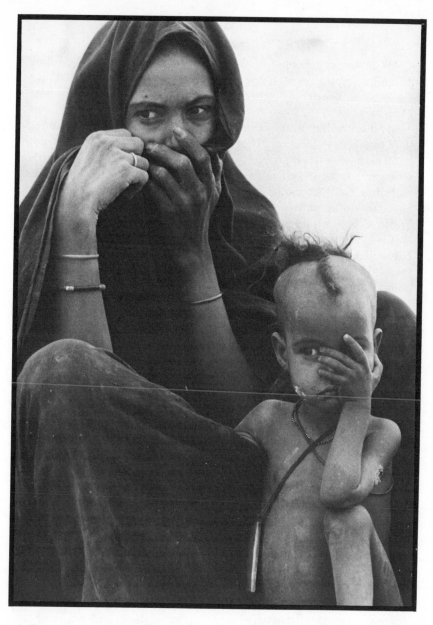

A five-year drought brought suffering and death to millions of people in the Sahel region of West Africa. This mother and child await help at a hospital in Agadez, Niger.
Photo taken in 1974. (UN/Gamma)

21

As an initial response, CWS helped with some of the feeding programs, mostly in Mali and Niger. It also contributed to a World Council of Churches consortium working in Upper Volta and Mauritania.

But its more important work in the Sahel, rehabilitation, came after the emergency feeding. The return of normal rainfall did not immediately solve all problems, of course. People needed to build a stronger economic system than they had before the drought. Some patterns developed earlier had proven unwise. In some areas, people had built up herds to a level that overloaded the ecological system. Future efforts would need to focus on more agricultural production.

A major contribution to the Sahel was Project Ladybug. People of Niger depended heavily on dates as a basic part of their diet. But an insect that covered leaves with a waxy scale was destroying the date palms. Scientists were brought in to devise ways to stem this destruction, but they found that when date offshoots were cut and taken to a different oasis for planting, scale insects went along comfortably while the ladybugs that normally kept them in check failed to survive the trip. So more ladybugs (actually, ladybeetles) were needed.

Date palms are thought to have originated in Mesopotamia, and scientists found a species of ladybugs in Iran that were extraordinarily effective against scale insects. Scientists from the Paris Museum of Natural History began trying them out in Mauritania, and a Nigerian who got training there went to Agadez, in central Niger, in 1972 and began setting ladybugs onto the date killers.

The next year, a young American who had gone to Niger with the Peace Corps, Philip Stansly, came upon this Nigerian, found him in need of funds and put him in touch with CWS. Then with CWS support, Mr. Stansly himself got into this biological war—*Lutte Biologique,* the French called it. After six weeks training in Mauritania, he began work in Tabelot, a remote village several hours north of Agadez.

Mr. Stansly was among the most colorful characters in CWS history. He identified with the culture of the Tuareg nomads to the extent of learning the tribal language, wearing tribal dress and marrying a Tuareg woman, whom he later brought to the United States. When he needed to go somewhere inaccessible by vehicle, this barefoot American in bright Tuareg robes set off on what became known as "the CWS camel."

The Iranian ladybug exhibited a voracious appetite for scale insects, devouring a hundred a day and making her value immediately visible to date growers. But keeping ladybugs in good health and abundantly reproductive presented difficulties. Hot dry spells set them back. As they devoured the scale insects, they were themselves devoured by birds. And discovering the best time of year for putting ladybugs onto the date palms required a period of experimentation.

Tohko Kaufmann, a scientist who had been working in the cocoa industry in Ghana, was enlisted to help work on these technical problems. In September 1975 she moved to Agadez, where she met such immediate challenges as electrical current that did not fit the light in her microscope. But pending arrival of a transformer, she used a makeshift arrangement of table lamps and mirrors.

A small, frail-looking woman approaching retirement age, she retained enough energy to spend all morning at her microscope and all afternoon in the field, despite 110-130 degree heat. A true international, she had been born in China to a Japanese mother and German father, and had secured a Ph.D. in entomology in Israel studying and doing field work in various parts of the world, from Israel to Alaska to Ghana.

Dr. Kaufmann discovered a mite previously unknown to biologists and named it for herself and CWS. This mite initially seemed even more effective than the ladybug in combatting scale insects, but scientists working at Agadez in later years found the mite's performance too erratic. So the ladybug remained the front line warrior in the *Lutte Biologique*.

Though the drought made outside aid even more crucial, CWS had been working in the Sahel for many years previously. From the 1950s it had aided school gardens. Teachers found that diet deficiency was keeping many children from learning, so they decided to create gardens beside the schools. They would produce food for the children while also providing practical education. This idea was carried out in several mission and government schools, with American churches providing seeds and tools and, later, well drilling equipment.

Then, after the drought killed off many of the cattle, the churches helped some of the nomads become settled farmers, and it brought in agronomists to assist them. Part of Philip Stansly's work was introducing improved varieties of potatoes and other vegetables in an Oasis Garden Program. He also helped the people improve their wells by cementing the walls. And he helped them organize farmers' cooperatives.

In 1975 CWS secured the services of Ralph and Flossie Royer,

23

As a result of agricultural development the people of the small village of Tabelot, which is part of the Oasis Air Project of CWS in Niger, now grow enough food for their own use, plus some for sale in Agadez.
Photo taken in 1979. (CWS photo/Hollon)

24

Church of the Brethren missionaries in Nigeria, and placed them in Agadez, a provincial government center for an area the size of France. While actually living in Agadez, the Royers provided technical skills to villagers in a remote area 90 miles north of Agadez. The work went on under the intriguing name, The Oasis Air Project.

Mr. Royer specializes in community development, particularly developing water resources. Like Philip Stansly, Ralph Royer speaks Housa, a trade language in use throughout that region. His rapport with the people developed quickly and so he was able to start assessing program needs immediately.

Most urgently, of course, they needed to grow food, so he helped these former nomadic cattle herders start gardens. Then to irrigate the gardens, he led them to the next step of drilling wells. But their gardens were intended to produce a cash crop as well as food for their own use, so Mr. Royer went on to a further educational step that trained them in weighing, computing value and other skills necessary for marketing in a more complex system than their traditional bartering.

As he moved from place to place, he next realized that the villages of an area needed some road linkage so growers could take their produce to a central farmer's market. He organized work crews that built 100 kilometers of road surveying the route on camels and using only hand tools to clear the land of rocks and bush. After that, the people cleared an area for a small airport so light airplanes could come in.

Moving step by step, from one evident need to the next, Mr. Royer led the people in a development program that became a show place for the nation. The result is that where people were virtually starving to death only a few years ago they now have adequate food to get them by and they are able to export a small amount of truck garden produce to Agadez for cash income. Besides that, they are self-supporting. At the height of the drought many of them were indebted to money-lenders who extracted an interest rate of 30% on money they loaned the people, who used it to buy food. Today when the President of Niger makes speeches about development, he cites this area as an example.

Elsewhere, CWS supported a variety of other projects to help people cope with the drought. In northern Kenya, it trained hundreds of Takanas, who had lost their herds, to do commercial fishing in Lake Rudolph. Some people in the Sahel were able to continue raising cattle and they were assisted with such projects as financing cattle dips to fight disease.

The Sahel, more than 95 per cent Muslim, had almost no church structure that an outside church agency could use as a local channel. At

Tchirozerine, 35 miles beyond Agadez, and still unconnected by road, a Belgian priest and a small group of French and Spanish sisters operated the only school for Tuaregs, a boarding school with 600 students. They had worked there since 1961, making no converts but seeking only to live out the presence of God. CWS representatives visited them and made a small grant to assist in the school operation.

But church mission programs had touched the Sahel in relatively few places. The entire country of Niger had only about 1000 Protestants and a few thousand Catholics, many of them government workers from Dahomey, Togo, Ivory Coast and Nigeria. So the common pattern of tying into national church life was impossible. But the Sahel program has helped create a better climate for the emergence of church life. And today a small Christian community is present, taking a responsible position in the life of its society and initiating projects that CWS seeks to support.

One of the few Protestants who have served in the Niger government is Mallam Diallo, a member of the small Protestant church in the Niger capital, Niamey. He was the one who first informed CWS of the school gardens project, and his daughter, Fatouma Diallo, has worked in the Niger office of CWS.

Experience in the Sahel drought has shown a need for a more alert international relief community, led by people committed to meeting need whenever it appears. A study sponsored by the Carnegie Endowment for International Peace was published in 1974 as *Disaster in the Desert: Failures of International Relief in the West African Drought.* It focused on the U.S. Agency for International Development (AID) and the UN Food and Agriculture Organization, charging that they neglected warnings of the impending crisis, and then moved ineffectively to counter its damage. The report charged that this failure, and a failure over the preceding decade to put significant sums into development of the Sahel, was due to a belief that the people there had little political importance.

In 1971, when UNESCO identified the 13 least developed countries of the world, the Sahel had four of them—Mali, Upper Volta, Chad and Niger –all with per capita annual income under $100 and adult literacy under 10 per cent. But despite the evident need, revealed in such facts as that Upper Volta and Niger were experiencing a negative growth rate, the people of this region received little development aid.

Another problem that became apparent in the Sahel, as it has in other areas, was the indifference that governments can show to the plight of their own people. Often, officials with the concern of the

26

Diallos seem conspicuously rare. How should an outside, voluntary agency act in the face of such an obstacle?

Sometimes the problem arises simply from governmental weakness. In the Sahel, government is often limited in its resources and capacity to deal with problems, even when there is a desire. It may have little contact with some areas and remain ill-informed about what is happening. Sometimes a government discourages publicity about a disaster for fear it will give the country a worse image. So if a weak and incompetent government exists in a country suffering from a disaster, it may show little reaction.

But beyond that, ruling groups often display lack of concern about what happens to powerless segments of their population. While many people were dying in the Sahel, others there were using irrigated land to raise beef for export.

This problem emerges in many places. As the churches seek to aid starving people, those controlling the land commonly use it to produce food for export to Western Europe and other affluent countries. These exports may enrich the small minority of landowners, who often include international corporations based in the United States or other developed countries, but leave the impoverished masses dependent on relief.

Nevertheless, it must be noted that after initial hesitancy the government of Niger gave what amounts to enthusiastic endorsement of the Oasis Air Project by assigning seven agricultural specialists to the project and enlarging their territory to include numerous villages scattered along a 70 mile network of dry river beds in the sub-Saharan desert floor.

Another problem is related to the attitudes of those who give aid and of those who receive it. When Americans provide relief, they are sometimes shocked to find that people of the receiving countries do not respond with unqualified gratitude, but often attack the United States for policies that they believe made the relief necessary. Part of the churches' job is helping interpret this response to American Christians.

A relief operation is only buying time so work can begin on fundamental problems. CWS believes it should not build up a permanent institutional presence in areas such as the Sahel, but that in any such operation it should plan to stay for at least two-to-four years.

It wants to stay long enough to make a difference. And the evidence shows that in the Sahel, it did make a difference.

4

Southern Africa—Lands of Decision

Africa has seen just about everything. She has seen her peoples exploited, enslaved, harassed, as she saw her wealth drained as well. Vast areas of this continent were divided like a great apple pie to be sliced up between the various western colonial powers. Over a five hundred year period one by one the western countries—Portugal, Belgium, France, Germany, Great Britain, Spain—all annexed parts of the continent and developed them to strengthen and expand their own economies. She has seen herself analyzed, scrutinized and categorized by political scientists, anthropologists and sociologists. In the past Africa was regarded as a deep, mysterious and silent continent, a riddle of the ages.

Today virtually all of our maps are out of date. Over thirty new nations have come into selfhood and self-governing authority. Instead of speaking of Africa as "Black Africa" we must speak of it as a continent exploding with life as everywhere one hears the sounds of the marching feet of new nations determined to create for their people a new and better life. Colonialism is almost extinct on the continent, and no where in the world is the Christian church more closely identified with the aspirations and the hopes of the people than in Africa where there are some of the fastest growing churches in the world.

The most common truth that one soon learns about Africa is that one cannot generalize about her. There is such great variety that little holds true for the entire continent or all of its people. There are many Africas. The olive groves of Tunisia are as much Africa as is the thick tangle of rain forest around the hospital that Albert Schweitzer built at

28

the turn of this century at Lambarene, Gabon. Cairo, Niamey, Gaborone, Nairobi and Durban are all African cities and each is different from the others. There are African tribes that still live in the Stone Ages and there are African painters whose abstractions hang in leading European galleries. A man who pilots giant earth-moving equipment by day may sleep in a thatch-roofed hut. He may have finished elementary school and be able to read little and write his own name but thanks to the transistor radio, which has found its way into the remotest corners of the country, he and his neighbors know a great deal about what is going on in the rest of the world.

Second only in size to Asia, Africa boasts almost 12 million square miles. She is more than three times the size of the continental United States and almost 5,000 miles long. Upwards of three hundred million people speaking eight hundred languages and dialects live in Africa. Her natural resources—gold, uranium, zinc, lead, iron, copper, diamonds, bauxite, petroleum and tin—remain largely untapped. This is Africa, vast and with a reserve of wealth that staggers the imagination. And now after centuries of being deliberately deprived and exploited by others, she is on a quest to find herself in the twentieth century.

As the winds of change blow across the African Continent no where is the change being felt greater than in southern Africa. Indeed rather than being a warm pleasant breeze it has reached violent gale force. Some feel that this is where Africa's future is being decided. Certainly it is where the last bastion of white supremecy is being challenged and shaken. Southern Africa includes South Africa, Namibia, Angola, Botswana, Lesotho, Swaziland, Mozambique, Malawi, Zimbabwe-Rhodesia and Zambia.

In a consultation held in Nairobi by the Division of Overseas Ministries (NCCC-USA) with African church leaders in 1979 the decision was made to make Africa and, particularly southern Africa, its top priority for 1980-82.

Unlike the Sahel the great strength of the Christian church in Africa is found in this southern region. These churches, once mission churches, are today self-governing autonomous churches and indeed there are many who feel that the churches in Africa are the fastest growing numerically in the whole world.

The recent history of southern Africa has been dominated by a struggle to end white minority rule and open the way for black determination. Though some churches, particularly the Dutch Reformed Church of South Africa, have defended white rule other

29

churches have taken a leading role in support of the majority black population. Because of the racial struggles the story of southern Africa has been in large part a story of refugees. Along with the traditional political and economic refugees southern Africa has produced a new category—educational refugees. Youngsters who have been denied educational opportunities in their own countries set out to find opportunity in other parts of the continent.

Botswana whose geography makes it a logical destination has received proportionately more refugees than any other country in the area. Adjacent to South Africa and Namibia it receives many refugees from the apartheid system installed there. In recent years it has taken in people fleeing from white rule in Angola, Mozambique and Rhodesia, and many of these.have remained in Botswana. Through the Botswana Council for Refugees an extension of the work of the Botswana Christian Council, American Christians have helped people such as Dean Michael Molale of the Anglican church in Botswana's capital city, Gaborone. A native of South Africa, Dean Molale studied in Zambia and England, and then accepted an invitation from the Bishop of Botswana to serve there. He has become a citizen of Botswana.

Dean Molale was particularly active and effective in helping the elementary and high school students who fled from Soweto, a suburb of Johannesburg, South Africa, after black protests there were suppressed by the authorities in 1976. He built a hostel in Gaborone for them to stay in, provided basic living necessities, and counseled them. Some of them eventually went back to their homes in Soweto.

American churches have assisted Botswana churches in developing job training programs for many of the refugees as well as for other people of that land. Agricultural schools train people in crop diversification and other skills to upgrade their food production. Other imaginative programs prepare young people for construction trades and another prepares them for managerial jobs in Howard Johnson-style motels that are being built in many African countries. The story of assistance to the churches of southern Africa is an exciting story, but it has not always been a very easy one to carry out because of the multiplicity of tribal loyalties and at times the overwhelming numbers of people who have needed help.

During the struggle for the independence of Mozambique from Portugal CWS assisted both FRELIMO (Mozambique Liberation Front) and COREMO (Coalition for Redemption and Education of Mozambique), a smaller competing liberation movement group,

Although they sometimes go unseen by the Western world, African refugees present dramatic witness to the conflicting currents of change moving across the continent.

(Gerard Klijn)

through such projects as assisting a hospital in Mombasa, Kenya to serve Mozambique refugees. Assistance also went to the Mozambique Institute in Dar es Salaam, Tanzania where many of the students would later become leaders of their country.

During the parallel struggle for Angola's independence from Portugal, food, blankets and cash grants were made available for needs in the north of Luanda through United Methodist Bishop Emilio de Carvalho for distribution to Angolans, and medical supplies were contributed to the mission hospitals in Angola. Sometimes Portuguese authorities allowed humanitarian assistance to enter legally. But at other times it had to be smuggled in from Zambia. For that enterprise, brigades of bicycle riders pedalled across the border and returned at night carrying aid from the outside. Medical assistance was offered to those in need through the southern part of Angola through medical stations staffed by medical mission personnel from North American staff of the United Church of Christ and the United Church of Canada.

When blacks from Zimbabwe-Rhodesia were forced to seek refuge in neighboring Mozambique and Zambia, aid went to them also. This aid included such products as grain, milk powder, clothing and blankets. It was all part of a determined effort to reach out to people in their great hour of need and to care for them and to give them hope in situations and times that seemed utterly hopeless.

In Zambia, where the Zimbabwe African People's Union operated camps for refugees, including large numbers of children, aid went to help with feeding and other basic needs.

Inside Zimbabwe-Rhodesia cash grants went to Christian Care, an organization formed by both black and white people to train young people in work brigades and to help retrain those who had been political detainees. In other words, instead of the church being a bystander on the side of the road watching people in their great hour of need and hurt, the church became involved in the lives of the people as is appropriate to its understanding of the gospel.

In Namibia CWS has had less direct involvement, but it did provide help through two Anglican Bishops, Donald Winter and Donald Wood, and then through the Namibian Council of Churches, formed in 1978. Lutheran World Relief has maintained a larger program because of the historical Lutheran presence there and the large Lutheran church membership dating back to the time when Namibia was South West Africa and governed as a German Colony. Through the many cooperative relationships maintained by the churches arrangements are often made for one denominational agency to take primary responsibility for a particular program and others then channel their aid through them. This was true when the Lutheran church undertook major assistance to refugees in Tanzania and the other American denominations sent their aid to them.

For a time in Vietnam the Mennonites acted on behalf of all the churches of the United States. When Hurricane David devastated much of the Caribbean in 1979, for example, the United Methodist Committee on Relief (UMCOR) acted on behalf of all the churches in helping Dominica.

In South Africa, CWS today helps support the work of several outstanding black church leaders. One of these is Bishop Desmond Tutu, former Anglican Bishop of Lesotho who has been general secretary of the South Africa Council of Churches since 1976. Church agencies of the United States and other countries channel money to the South Africa Council through the World Council of Churches' Commission on Inter-Church Aid, Refugee and World Service (CICARWS).

This helps support both the general work of the Council and its unit on Inter-Church Aid and Service, which helps the churches conduct programs of agricultural development and assistance to new communities. When the government moves blacks onto bantustans where they have no adequate means of support, Bishop Tutu helps supply the basic help they need to begin a new community life.

Grants to the South Africa Council also help support work in community organization and counseling with Soweto youth. The South Africa Women's Union organizes domestic workers and holds conferences for black women to talk about their role in an oppressive society. Grants help buy education materials for these programs.

CWS also supports the work of the Cape Colored Women's Association. A worker goes from house to house in the colored (mixed ancestry) community, talking with the women whose husbands are away for long periods doing contract labor. The worker teaches reading to those who are illiterate, offers other forms of basic education and seeks in various ways to help keep families together. The worker also trains other people to do the same kind of work.

Annual grants go to the Asingini Fund, which provides legal aid to South Africans in jail or threatened with jail because of their resistance to apartheid. And CWS supports the Dependents Conference, which aids families of detainees. Often, fathers are imprisoned and large families are left with no income. The Dependents Conference helps with school fees and other family needs.

Women in a training program in Zambia take a break for tea.

The struggle in southern Africa is not only against white minority rule, but also against poverty. American churches join this struggle as supporters of development. They assist the Malawi Christian Service Committee and its program of community organization, health care and well drilling. In Botswana, they support rural dental programs. In Zambia, they support the Mindolo Ecumenical Foundation and its work in vocational training.

Another aspect of the program in southern Africa has been helping black liberation groups get into dialogue with each other and with the outside world. This work is often done cooperatively by churches of many countries working through national and regional councils and the World Council. Where a single country has competing groups, such as South Africa with its African National Congress and Pan-African Congress, the churches have helped bring them together for discussion of their differences. Such efforts, though not always successful in resolving the differences, serve to reduce misunderstanding and diminish the level of internal conflict in the black community.

In 1976, when a major conference, ultimately unsuccessful, was held in Geneva to attempt a Rhodesian settlement, the churches helped pay expenses for representatives of the black liberation groups that might not have been able to go otherwise. Churches provided similar assistance for the more successful 1979 conference in London.

Included in this work is a great deal of simple humanitarian aid to people caught up in a struggle that is not the romantic adventure it sometimes appears. In 1978 when many representatives of African organizations were assassinated in civil unrest, church assistance enabled widows and other family members to attend the funerals which were sometimes held in neighboring countries.

CWS also acts directly in advocacy work on behalf of justice for blacks in southern Africa. It calls on the U. S. government to conduct a foreign policy more responsive to the demands of justice. And it calls on corporations doing business in southern Africa to operate in accordance with principles of corporate responsibility.

None of this means that American churches are endorsing the specific agenda of any liberation group, the violence in which its members may engage or the political ideology they espouse. Still less do the American churches think they should decide which groups will represent blacks of southern Africa, or determine what their strategy will be.

But the churches supporting CWS do endorse the concepts of social

35

justice and black self-determination. So they stand by in support of African churches as they participate in the struggles of their people.

At the African Emphasis Consultation held in April 1979 in Nairobi one action of the Consultation participants was the issuance of an appeal to the Vatican, the general secretary of the World Council of Churches, the general secretary of the U.S. National Council of Churches and other Christian leaders:

"With deep sadness and emotion we listened to the declaration of our South African sisters as they asked us to pray for the white South African community which is imprisoned by fear and hatred. We were impressed with their conviction that all was not irretrievably lost between the black and white communities in South Africa."

"We believe that if an action were undertaken by the worldwide Christian community toward the churches of South Africa that the result would be the opening of new dialogue."

"We therefore make an appeal to you in your position of leadership in the worldwide Christian community to organize a 'Week of Prayer and Action' on the South African situation. The date should be set so as to be common throughout the world."

"We suggest that the 'Week of Prayer and Action' should be preceded by a global campaign in which information on the South African situation is shared."

After asking that parishes and denominations write letters to South African parishes, the South African Council of Churches and the writers' own governments, the appeal concludes:

"We firmly believe that such a concerted, global Christian action with prayer, directed towards the Christian community in South Africa, would help to change the present direction of an increasingly tragic situation."

A broad concept of what development means was outlined in "Directions from Nairobi," the report published after the consultation. It began with the declaration:

"The task that confronts us as African and American brothers and sisters working together is enormous. It entails nothing less than the liberation of us all from exploitative, degrading and oppressive structures and from the bondage of poverty; of the establishment of a just and equitable social, economic and political order; and of the full development of opportunities for people to live in dignity, security and health with the chance to achieve their God-granted 'Fulness of Humanity.' This task binds us together in fidelity to our common Lord and to the imperative He left with us."

"The development that we work for together," the document continued, "implies not only the securing of basic and important human needs but also the opportunity for the complete fulfillment of the individual in all dimensions. Development under the sovereignty of God involves a reverence for the earth as God's creation and a quest for the wholeness of human beings.

"Development entails a process of becoming responsible for one's own life, livelihood and environment. Development involves an enhancement of self-awareness, self-determination and self-reliance. It is too significant a dimension of our life together to be left to secular institutions alone. It must be an integral part of our common Christian witness in our work and in our institutions."

"Directions from Nairobi" gave special attention to southern Africa, and said the struggle for development and human fulfillment in other parts of the continent must "always be viewed against the backdrop of the struggle of our southern African brothers and sisters for liberation." This was called a "foremost priority."

Consultation participants saw the task of U. S. churches not merely in contributing funds and other support for programs in Africa, but also in educating their U. S. constituency about the need for change in their government's policies affecting Africa.

In addition to discussion of basic principles of development, the Consultation produced a list of special concerns for the continent of Africa:

—refugees, of whom Africa currently has "millions," and their numbers are increasing. Along with immediate relief aid, they need the long term services of resettlement or voluntary repatriation, and job training.

—development planning and administration. A task that should be undertaken by each national council of churches.

—rural development, food production and water resources. Areas of "crucial" concern for the churches since most people of Africa still live in rural areas.

—primary health care. An effort to bring health care into the villages where it is currently lacking.

—technical assistance and appropriate technology. Features that release time and energy for further human development.

—inter-religious dialogue and, wherever possible, cooperation in development. This is particularly important with regard to Muslims.

—communication and interchange. Activities that enable the churches to accomplish their mission.

No where in the Third World is the church more actively involved seeking to make its witness for Jesus Christ in the proclamation of the good news; of seeing lives transformed by God's power; seeing clenched fists slowly opened to become hands of blessing. But also the church has moved into the arena of great controversy at times, seeking to be faithful to its lord and master, seeking to be sensitive to human need wherever it has been confronted by it. In all of these tasks the American churches have their role not to direct the planning but to be partners with Africans in this great task of healing, reconciliation and overthrowing of cruelty systems, confronting man's inhumanity to his fellow man.

5

Indochina: Nationalism—Holocaust—Refugees

The occasion was a gathering of several hundred church people at a conference in the Midwest. I had just returned from one of many visits to Vietnam. The war was still raging. Nearly 500,000 American troops were locked in combat with the North Vietnamese and tensions were running high across our nation.

At the end of the presentation, during which I had spoken of the heroic struggles of the people in South Vietnam to find a way of peace and justice, of the endless stream of refugees pouring south into the delta, there was a time for question. At the back of the church a man rose to his feet and called out, "We heard you speak tonight so eloquently about Vietnam and Indochina, now I really want to know an honest answer to one question. The question is 'Are you a hawk or are you a dove?' "

Those were the days when it seems as if the whole nation was divided into one or two camps. I paused for a moment realizing perhaps that this was a no-win question because no matter which side I spoke to there would be a large number who would disagree.

In despair I said, "Well I guess I'll have to say that on the subject of Vietnam and this bloody, endless war, I am strickly chicken." Tension in the church lowered. Some wondered if my answer had been facetious but really it was a question of fear; fear for own people, fear for the people of Vietnam. I had walked across the rice fields, trudged through endless refugee camps in South Vietnam and the poignancy of it all was perhaps symbolized by a beautiful teenage girl sitting on the end of the hospital bed in Nahtrang. As I looked into the face of this lovely young Vietnamese girl it seemed to me that if she had lived in

39

Tenafly, N.J. rather than Nahtrang, South Vietnam she could have been one of the high school cheer leaders at a Saturday afternoon high school football game.

Instead, as I looked down at her I saw both her legs had been amputated after stepping on a land mine. My question perhaps was the wrong question to her. I simply asked," What are you going to do?"

Through an interpreter her reply still haunts me. "I don't know."

What else could she say for her own future seemed so uncertain? The days of those two questions seem now removed by many years from the scene tonight in 1980. This morning Church World Service staff cleared all the necessary documentation for another chartered DC 10 cargo jet out of Bangkok to airlift another 25 tons of medicine and urgently needed food into Phnon Penh, Kampuchea.

After 30 years of suffering such as the world has rarely seen, the mass media daily remind us that with Kampuchea the world has witnessed, without realizing it, what Ellie Wiesel, survivor of Dachau and the Holocaust, has described as the second holocaust. As God looked down upon Europe in 1940-45 he must have wept at the sight of millions of people who were perishing in Hitler's gas ovens. But then 50% of Kampuchea today has perished from the earth; slaughtered and starved to death by one of the most ruthless regimes of the 20th century—the regime of Pol Pot. Will it ever end? Will the suffering of these gentle people of Indochina ever come to a conclusion, so that refugees can once again go home; lives can be rebuilt and the once fertile rice fields of Indochina, the orchards and farms, provide once again all the food that is needed to maintain this part of Southeast Asia?

These and a thousand other questions break in upon us as we try to show our caring and our sharing in responding to human need. Prior to the Vietnam war, the mainline Protestant churches of United States had never worked in Indochina, while they had poured literally thousands of missionaries into China, Thailand, Malaysia, Indonesia and the Philippines, all close neighbors of Vietnam. This was one area which one small American church had been left alone to relate to in the last 100 years and yet Indochina was to be the area where CWS would conduct one of its largest and most multifaceted programs in its entire history. American involvement in the Vietnam War focused attention there and forced the churches to think about their responsibility to the unparalleled suffering of people caught in the war.

Never since the Civil War had Americans been so divided. The debates became heated and bitter as the United States went from

Vietnamese fleeing from Saigon, later renamed Ho Chi Minh City, during the Tet offensive.
(Wide World Photo)

limited involvement with "military advisers" to massive and active participation by American troops, with a loss of more than 50,000 American lives and at the same time over 1 million Vietnamese and Laotians. Controversy continued to rage through the period of prolonged withdrawal, eventual communist take-overs in Vietnam, Laos and Cambodia and efforts to deal with the aftermath of war. Three years after the last American troops had been evacuated from Vietnam, and like an ugly dream of a painful illness from which the patient has recovered, it seemed as if Vietnam had passed into the recesses of our attention.

There were other areas of the world now demanding our concern. Suddenly, almost overnight, once again America was to be involved as refugees started pouring out of Indochina. 132,000 had come to our land at the end of the American Vietnamese military operations and now hundreds of thousands more began to seek sanctuary in other countries as droughts struck rice fields of Indochina resulting in widespread hunger. New efforts by the government of Vietnam to create a single nation; the almost unknown shadow-like destruction of Kampuchea by Pol Pot; and new uprisings in Laos added to the total. These refugees came by land across the frontier of Laos and Cambodia into Thailand.

Others were visibly risking their lives to escape in small boats into the South China Sea. How many thousands have perished at sea will remain forever unknown. Many of these boats, when they were fortunate enough to reach a neighboring country, were pushed back out to sea by the people of that country fearful that their own way of life would be threatened by this peaceful "invasion." The world saw maritime ships openly violating the law of the sea in passing by the "boat people" in distress, a shocking result of the refusal of other countries in the area to let the ships discharge Vietnamese it had saved from drowning.

Cambodia was really a "sideshow" to the Vietnam conflict but now produced such grisly stories as to force it into the center of the world's attention. By the end of 1979 over half a million Indochinese were destitute in refugee camps, a symbol of man's inhumanity to his fellow man. Thailand, Malaysia, Indonesia, the Philippines and Hong-Kong, inundated by these new refugees, appealed to the world for assistance to move them out. Even now over 80% of these refugees, many of whom have been waiting in camps for over 4 years, continue to live in despair, longing for that moment when someone will tell them: "You can leave. There is a country waiting to receive you."

42

Through all these turns of the wheels of history one thing remained constant: the commitment of the American churches through CWS to do whatever it could in meeting human need.

For a four year period after a 1954 victory of Ho Chi Minh and his Vietnamese forces over the French at Dienbienphu, CWS was to send food and relief supplies to refugees fleeing from North to South. But its member denominations had no continuing involvement in Vietnam and its program ended after the accomplishment of its initial sending of aid.

Christians formed only a tiny minority in Vietnam, and as a result of the French colonial background which heavily favored Roman Catholic missions and made it virtually impossible for Protestant missionaries to work, the Christian population was 95% Roman Catholic. The work of missionaries from the Christian Missionary Alliance in the United States had brought into being a small Protestant church called Tin Lanh. The first of these missionaries visited Vietnam in 1893 and they established a mission in 1911. By 1975 the Tin Lanh church had some 50,000 members, but all other Protestants of the country numbered less than 7,000 combined. Church World Service's decision to return to Vietnam in a long term program of aid at the height of the Vietnam war came through its partner the Mennonite Central Committee. When typhoons killed 7,000 Vietnamese and left 700,000 homeless in November 1964, CWS gave food, blankets, clothing and funds to the Mennonites for use in relief.

But as the American military presence in Vietnam grew, as the war disrupted the lives of millions of Vietnamese people, as Americans focussed their attention on this previously little known region, the time had come for the churches to undertake a major effort of relief and rehabilitation. So by a memorandum of understanding dated January 6, 1966 CWS joined with the Mennonite Central Committee and Lutheran World Relief to form Vietnam Christian Service (VNCS), an agency which would serve as its primary vehicle in Vietnam for the next 9 years.

This aid was expressed primarily through the services of skilled personnel who came to minister to the hurts of these people and to demonstrate the compassion of God's people for their neighbors. However, VNCS as it began to distribute food provided by the U.S. government found this food program too closely linked with American political goals in Vietnam and so it withdrew from this kind of involvement. Gradually VNCS was to become the largest operation in which CWS was to participate anywhere in the world. At one point there were 90 staff members in addition to over 200 Vietnamese. Teachers, doctors, nurses, social workers, physiotherapists, argricul- turalists, irrigation experts—these were some of the skilled people needed for an effective assistance to the people of South Vietnam.

Their work developed in stages according to the changing military and political situation. At first, during the heaviest U.S. military involvement the emphasis was on helping victims of the war, particularly those among the hundreds of thousands of refugees who had fled from North Vietnam and who later had been dislodged from their homes along the coastal plains of South Vietnam. The emphasis after 1973, when the United States withdrew militarily with the signing of the peace treaty until the fall of the Saigon government in April 1975, was on training Vietnamese to perform the various services of the agency. Two young physiotherapists from southern California were representatives of many of the VNCS staff. Recruited for a two year assignment,they were sent to Saigon not to work in a hospital as physiotherapists themselves, although this need was very urgent, but they were told that in the 2 years their assignment would be to reproduce their training in the lives of 12 young Vietnamese women so that at the end of their term of service there would be 12 physiotherapists to work in the crowded hospitals. The training of social workers, nurses, paramedics became high priorities with realization that the time was soon coming when an outside person would no longer be accepted in Vietnam.

In the closing days of the conflict, as the Saigon government became less and less able to provide security, VNCS was compelled to reduce the scope of its activity. After the murder of a key American staff member in the highlands, with the attack on a rural hospital, these areas had to be abandoned and yet despite these serious setbacks and the ending of the official U.S. presence in Vietnam in April 1975, plans were already in the making in a consultation with colleague churches in 'Western Europe, Australia, New Zealand and Canada to begin an outreach of reconciliation and justice. Despite the fact that all foreign personnel had to leave the area, the World Council of Churches launched the Fund for Reconciliation and Reconstruction in Indochina (FRRI), and CWS provided major support to this program. In its initial phase, the FRRI raised $10 million for work in North and South Vietnam, Laos and Cambodia.

"The FRRI grew out of the long and painful search," wrote Earnest Fogg the director of the fund, "not only for answers but of the right questions in the tragedy of Indochina."

Churches had not been alone in that search. They had been vulnerable in their comfortable and familiar role of good Samaritan. They were expected to engage in acts of mercy but responsibility for national and international political decisions could not be shrugged off. These decisions were more than abberations of individual political administrations when they were supported by large numbers of Christians.

On February 22, 1975, fifty-five Christian leaders, twenty from Asia and thirty-five from the rest of the world, including staff and directors of CWS, met in Vientiane, Laos to plan the program of reconciliation and reconstruction in the three countries that constitute Indochina. Nguyen Tang Canh, the Vietnamese staff member of the Fund for Reconstruction and Reconciliation, reported to the group, "Millions of dislocated people have been forced to live in unfamiliar places and to accept different social and moral standards, these new practices have often violated traditional customs and morality. There have been in South Vietnam alone over 200,000 more casualties. American children number twenty to thirty thousand depending on who is making the estimate. There are an estimated 1,000,000 orphans. Refugee families have crowded into the cities. Widows, orphans, the handicapped, the disabled war veterans are so numerous that the combined efforts of the government and the voluntary agencies have not been adequate to meet their needs."

He continued, "Prostitution, drug addiction, black marketeering have been reduced by the withdrawal of foreign troops, yet the war has dealt a blow to moral values, and traditional behavior. Political prisoners number 100,000 to 300,000 depending on the source. Continued imprisonment of people for political attitudes is a moral problem for the nation. The attitude of mistrust and suspicion is inimicable to reconciliation. Hate propaganda is broadcast and fomented by psycho-war teams. The people are frightened and confused. Factionalism paralyzes the many groups and organizations committed to reconstruction."

That the churches around the world made a very effective contribution in reconstruction in Vietnam following the end of the war is now a matter of record. But the failure of the churches to carry out a program of reconciliation was in part rooted in the problem that the Vietnamese government saw reconciliation as a political word and not as a humanitarian word. So, Dr. Robert MacAfee Brown, in 1975 at the consultation in Vientiane, Laos had said to us, "If Americans feel guilty about the war in Vietnam there is a great deal for which we are guilty. American guns, American tanks, American rockets, American napalm, American bombers, American flame throwers and American arrogance, brought the destruction out of which we must now seek reconstruction and reconciliation. This particular American, at least, must ask himself why should Indochina want any Americans in these countries we have so ravaged? Why should they not want us to get out and leave them alone? After the 'kind of help' we have given over the last decade how can they possibly trust us today or want us to make any contribution to their future? What we Americans have done has created deep enmity between Americans and Indochinese. How, under these circumstances, can there be reconciliation?"

He concluded by saying to the gathering, which included representatives from Vietnam, Laos and Cambodia, "I speak as I have only because truth can serve the cause of truth, because those of you who share my Christian faith know that what binds us together in the faith is far deeper than what separates us nationally, geographically or ideologically, and finally, because those of you who share with me a common humanity, and that includes all of us, knows that speaking across divisions which threaten that humanity is the only certain way to build bridges of understanding that can unite us."

In November 1978 the World Council began a new effort with the first meeting of the Indochina Consortium which agreed to seek $2 million for an agricultural program in Laos and $2 million for the Lam Dong New Economic Zone in the Vietnamese highlands. The latter was expected to provide a place for 100,000 people from North Vietnam.

Meanwhile, the American churches' own Indochina program continued along two tracks. One was continued aid to refugees. Church World Service began through its member churches to find sponsors across the United States to bring the Indochina refugees out of the camps and to help them rebuild their lives again. The second track of the American churches' Indochina program was a CWS effort to promote reconciliation and friendship between the peoples of Vietnam and the United States. This involved sending delegations, shipping food for relief, providing agricultural equipment to increase Vietnam's capacity to feed itself and serving as an advocate in the United States for normalized diplomatic and trade relations with Vietnam.

A special chapter in the Indochina program of this period was sending a ship with 10,000 tons of American wheat to Vietnam. On April 2, 1978, this ship sailed, the first one to go from the United States

Wheat from the United States, sent by CWS to Vietnam as an act of reconciliation, is bagged by hand before unloading.
(CWS photo)

directly to Vietnam after the war had ended. The shipment of wheat was intended to go beyond supplying food, which had been done earlier by shipments of rice purchased in Asia, and was to serve as a gesture of reconciliation. In Houston, Texas a group of CWS officials and friends gathered on the grounds of the Rothko Chapel for a service of dedication. The program included gospel and country music and the Houston Jazz Ballet. One by one, six people stepped up to the platform, poured grain into a large basket symbolizing the wheat shipment and explained what the shipment meant.

"I represent the farmers who grew the wheat," said Harvey Schmidt of Kansas, "and rather than plow it under, we give it to the Vietnamese, for they need it."

"I represent CROP," said Ann Taylor, "who made the arrangements to collect this wheat and ship it by rail to Houston."

"I represent the organizations that endorsed this shipment," said Cliff Kirkpatrick of Houston Metropolitan Ministries, "and give this wheat as a gesture of reconciliation between the peoples of our two nations."

"I give this wheat because the children of the world are friends," said Susan Ross, a 13-year-old resident of Houston.

Dick Clark, who was then a U.S. Senator from Iowa and member of the Agriculture and Foreign Relations Committees, gave the main address. "This grain becomes a symbol, important even beyond the value of the food dedicated here today," he said. "It is a symbol that says to the world that the American people understand the needs of those who are hungry and who need help. It is a symbol that the Vietnam War is over."

Senator Hubert H. Humphrey of Minnesota had endorsed the shipment shortly before his death. And 17 other senators signed a letter he circulated calling on President Carter to share surplus American wheat and rice with Vietnam and Laos.

The service in Houston included the reading of a message from Coretta Scott King:

"Let us pray that ships of wheat will turn swords into ploughshares, and that your initiative will be heard in Congress . . . and that many ships will follow so that our workers will have jobs and our people may prosper from your example of hands reaching for peace."

For CWS, relationships always take precedence over projects. It thinks first of building relationships, and of choosing projects that will serve this goal. Such projects as the wheat shipment have helped the agency build relationships in Vietnam following the war and have enabled it to do other work as a consequence of the trust it has established.

One of the most significant results of this trust and acceptance has been a series of highly significant conversations between CWS staff and directors and the leaders of the Protestant churches and the Catholic Bishops in North and South Vietnam. Several memorable conversations have taken place as Vietnamese and American church people worshiped together.

As these lines are being written a letter just crossed my desk from the President of the Tin Lanh (Protestant Church of Vietnam representing the entire Protestant Christian community).

> "Our days of isolation are over. We expect within a few months to be a full member church of the Christian Conference of Asia. We look forward to a new day of relationships with our brothers and sisters in Christ across Asia."

Just a few years ago such a decision would have been thought utterly impossible.

The Vietnamese government agreed in 1979 that the United Nations High Commissioner for Refugees could open an office in Ho Chi Minh City (Saigon) to assist citizens to immigrate to the United States and other parts of the world for family reunification. Michael and Sarah Myers, the son and daughter-in-law of veteran China missionaries, were loaned by CWS to the U.N. office to assist in this work. They were the first representatives of any U.S. voluntary agency allowed to work in Vietnam since the war ended.

Vietnam drove Pol Pot from Phnom Penh in 1979 and set up a new government under Heng Samrin. CWS on October 26, 1979 launched a $5 million campaign from its member churches for Kampuchea relief. It began organizing a coalition of U.S. agencies to work in Kampuchea and opened an office in Phnom Penh to work cooperatively with the World Council Commission on Interchurch Aid Refugees and World Service, the United Nations, and the Kampuchean government. A new ministry which demonstrates our concern by providing urgently needed relief has begun.

The appeal of $5 million within a very short time was fully subscribed. And once again plans are now in the making not just for a short term relief operation but for a long term commitment to help the people of Kampuchea rebuild their homes and their lives. The resources of CWS and its member churches are not equal to the enormity of need nor to the resources available through intergovernmental agencies, but our resolve is there in Kampuchea as it was years ago in Saigon to say to the people of that land in the name of God, "we do care."

So the Indochina chapter cannot be concluded here. It began in 1954, providing food for refugees fleeing from North to South Vietnam and 26 years later it faces an unfinished task.

In Vientiane, Laos the Mennonite Central Committee has a young couple, the son and daughter-in-law of a former veteran CWS staff member, living in that city as a visible sign of our caring and search for reconciliation. Doug Beane, another CWS veteran who also worked with the Vietnamese Christian Service in Vietnam, with his Vietnamese wife is now based in Bangkok, Thailand where he serves as CWS Indochina Liasion staff person. Steve Collins, a young man who worked with CWS in Haiti, has gone to Phnom Penh, Kampuchea to monitor the shipments of supplies coming in from the six U.S. voluntary agencies in the Action for Relief and Rehabilitation in Kampuchea (ARRK) coalition. Michael Lynch, a CARE staff member is the acting field director for ARRK in Kampuchea. And the Myers are in Ho Chi Minh City helping to reunite families long divided by the dispersion resulting from the war.

There are still no diplomatic relationships between United States and Vietnam and the only American representative in that country has been sent by the church as an agent of reconciliation. We the recipients of God's reconciliation must be instruments of God's reconciliation to others. The Christian is concerned not only that we be reconciled to God but also to one another. There is no reconciliation with God that does not include reconciliation with brother and sister. No wonder that the reconciliation claim of Christians appears unbelievable to non-Christians but the commitment to go on helping in Indochina remains one of the highest priorities of Church World Service in the years ahead.

6

Middle East—Crossroads of Destiny

Jerusalem—Bethlehem—Nazareth—Antioch—Rome. These are names that strike a familiar chord to everyone of us because from our childhood they have been part of our biblical heritage. Today in the mass media we are learning a new geography of the Middle East. To most of us the names are unfamiliar, Abu Dhabi—Dubai—Muscat—Oman—Kuwait—Saudi Arabia. These are new centers of world power because the continued prosperity of most of the western world and the very existence of much of the third world depends on what is known in the Middle East as "Black Gold," or to us, simply, oil.

The three major monotheistic religions of the Middle East, Judaism, Christianity and Islam, all had their birth and early history there. In contrast to the Sahel where there is virtual absence of churches and southern Africa where there are relatively young but rapidly growing churches, the Middle East has given CWS an opportunity to join forces with churches that trace their history to the apostles. Churches established in apostolic times have a continued life and presence in the Middle East ever since. According to their traditions a number of them claim specific founders: James in Jerusalem; Peter and Paul in Antioch and Rome; Thomas in Babylonia; Mark in Alexandria and Barnabas in Cyprus. There is a tremendous stirring in these churches which for long centuries lived a minority existence under the Muslim rulers of that area of the world. Most people have commonly thought of the Arab world as Muslim and further, have seen the Middle East as a Muslim area in conflict with the people of Israel. We need to be reminded that the Arab world also inclues some 14 million Christians.

The Middle East is a vast stretch of land extending from Afghanistan

51

to the shores of Mauritania on the Atlantic. The 19 countries that make up this great area with 150 million people are characterized by differing historical origins, traditions, and languages, even though the dominant religion is Islam. A few of these countries possess much of the world's oil resources. The people of the Middle East are now at a crossroads. They must adjust to changing conditions, choose between conflicting loyalties, as they struggle to find their own particular destiny. For nearly 30 years Church World Service and its member denominations have provided financial and material support for programs involving the Palestinian refugees. When conflicts first erupted in Palestine in 1948 and again in 1956, 1967, 1973, and more recently in Lebanon the churches' programs were geared towards providing relief, reconciliation and rehabilitation to answer immediate and desperate needs. These have been followed by long-range development programs aimed at raising hopes for a better future for these people.

The churches of the Middle East have been confronted by a number of problems throughout their history. They have to a considerable extent found themselves isolated from the rest of the Christian world. Whereas today the role of the western churches is a very positive one, assisting these churches to minister to the needs of their own people and to their Muslim neighbors, experience in the past in their contact with the West was often negative. Western Christians have come in modern times as crusaders, most conspicuously as representatives of colonial powers. Mission efforts have often been misunderstood and appeared to residents of the Middle East as a religious dimension of colonialism. Today Church World Service tries to establish relationships between the American and Middle East churches that will to some degree redress this legacy. It seeks to strengthen the work of the Middle East churches. Rather than conduct programs of its own it provides resources so the churches established in the area can become more effective servants of their own society.

Through the years, CWS has developed working relationships with many of the outstanding church leaders of the Middle East. In 1960, a United Church of Christ layperson, Richard Butler, was employed by the Congregational Christian Service Committee and seconded to CWS for work in the Middle East. There he met a Lebanese layperson of the Antiochian Orthodox Church, Gabriel Habib, and established ties that grew in importance as Mr. Butler became Middle East director for CWS and Mr. Habib became general secretary of the Middle East Council of Churches.

Mr. Habib, called Gabi (Gabby) by his friends, got his first ecumenical experience working with the World Council's Commission on Inter-Church Aid, Refugee and World Service (CICARWS) in Tunisia after the French departed. Then he became Middle East representative of the World Council's youth department, based in Beirut. At the same time he served as general secretary of the Orthodox youth organization, Syndesmos, and as Middle East secretary for the World Student Christian Federation.

In the 1970s, Mr. Habib joined the staff of the Middle East Council of Churches. The history of this Council goes back to the 1920s when John R. Mott held a series of "Muslim Christian Conferences" leading up to a general conference in Jerusalem in 1924. Participants in the Jerusalem conference proposed the establishment of an area council, which was organized in 1927 and, from 1929, called the Near East Christian Council.

In the beginning, its membership was entirely Protestant. Most of its leaders were missionaries oriented to mission work among Muslims or, in some cases, proselytizing from Orthodox churches. But the situation changed as relations between Protestant and Orthodox churches of the world later grew warmer. At the 1961 Assembly in New Delhi, the World Council of Churches received several more Orthodox churches into its membership, and during the same Assembly completed a merger with the International Missionary Council. These developments had effects in the Middle East, where the Christian Council began seeking ways of becoming more ecumenical. A first step was changing its name in 1964 to Near East Council of Churches and making it an organization whose members no longer included foreign mission boards but only churches of the area.

Since 1948, a primary impetus to increased Christian cooperation in the Middle East has been concern for Palestinian refugees. Major conferences on this topic were held in 1951 and 1956. But the 1967 War exacerbated the problem of refugees, and moved Middle East churches toward an increased willingness to work cooperatively on their behalf.

Another conference, held in the Cyprus capital, Nicosia, in 1969, brought two important developments. It led immediately, in 1970, to establishment of the Near East Ecumenical Committee for Palestine Refugees. And it helped bring about a later reorganization and expansion of the Council. In May 1974, the Near East Council was dissolved, and 22 Eastern Orthodox, Oriental Orthodox, Anglican and Protestant churches in 14 countries formed the Middle East Council of Churches.

This Palestinian family has set up housekeeping in a camp in east Jordan.
(UNRWA/Nehmeh)

The Committee for Palestine Refugees became the Council's Department on Service to Palestine Refugees. Though the Council established its headquarters in Beirut, the Service Department remained in Nicosia, and was conveniently placed to help Greek Cypriots who became refugees after the Turkish occupation of Northern Cyprus later in 1974.

CWS has never conducted a separate program of its own for Palestinian refugees, but has assisted area programs that have continued under various structures and now operate under the Middle East Council. Mr. Butler emphasizes, however, that the relationship with the Council and leaders such as Mr. Habib is not a matter only of giving assistance. "We have gained more from Gabi than he has from us," he says. The relationship is one of American Christians learning to understand more about the nature of the Middle East conflict, and more about their brother and sister Christians there.

Mr. Butler notes that the experience of Middle East Christians as members of a minority may turn out to be something Western Christians will need to learn from in the future if secularism continues to increase its dominance over Western culture.

One way CWS tries to help Palestinians is by interpreting their cause to American Christians and the general public. Within the National Council of Churches, efforts to support the cause of Palestinian rights have created some tension. The Council is also committed to strengthening Christian-Jewish relations, and the two programs do not easily harmonize.

But through its personal relationships with Middle East Christians, CWS has come to believe that the Palestinians have a just claim on the world's conscience, and on the conscience of American Christians. What it has learned through its Middle East relationships, and what it has sought to tell American Christians, is summarized in a 1977 statement of Sami Habiby, chairperson of the Service Department:

"For most Palestinians, prospects remain bleak after 30 years of dispersion and destitution. Many in the West echo Israel's expedient call for the resettlement of the refugees in the Arab world. But the Palestinians themselves reject the argument that a people evicted from a homeland to which they remain passionately attached should be shunted off elsewhere for the convenience of those largely responsible for their situation. For we believe that the West is greatly responsible for what is called the Middle East problem.

"Given the premise that the only lasting solution to the Middle East conflict lies in recognizing the legitimate national rights and aspirations of the people of Palestine, what is the role of concerned Western Christians in achieving this goal? First and foremost, we expect them to share with us in exercising the Christian faculties of love, justice and charity, and to try to achieve empathy with the Palestinians in their struggle for recognition and restitution.

"In the meantime, we expect Western Christians to recognize their responsibility towards fellow human beings whose sufferings are so largely due to the working out of international politics. They should understand that the vast majority of Palestinians, while grateful for all help extended to them, are particularly interested in assistance towards helping themselves prepare for that time—however near or distant—when they will be full citizens in their own country, with all the responsibilities that implies.

"There is another, more parochial reason for Western Christians to be concerned and generous: already, Christians constitute the bulk of Palestinian emigrants to the West since they find it easier to assimilate than their Muslim brothers. Should the Palestinian Christian community disappear through neglect, the last living links tying the Christian West to the land of Christ will be broken, leaving the Christian holy places in the Holy Land to decline into mere museums and tourist traps."

Palestinians number a little more than three million. There are about one million in Jordan, 750,000 on the West Bank, 400,000 each in Lebanon, Israel and Gaza, 200,000 in Syria and smaller numbers in other Middle East countries. Also many Palestinians have emigrated to other parts of the world.

The Service Committee operates through area committees for Lebanon, Jordan, Israel, Gaza and the West Bank. For example, the International Christian Committee in Jerusalem serves as area committee for the West Bank. Its executive secretary, Elias Khoury, a Palestinian Christian of the Orthodox Patriarchate of Jerusalem, carries responsibility for village development, vocational training and other West Bank projects.

Another area committee supervises a program to help Egyptians who were displaced from the Suez region after the 1967 War and returned when Israel withdrew in 1975. Much of the housing had been destroyed by shelling from 1967 to 1970, and efforts were undertaken to help them secure temporary shelter. A hostel was opened for single women, who were also offered courses in literacy, health education, home economics and handicrafts. Another hostel was opened for men.

In addition to the Middle East Council, refugee activities of the

YWCA in Jerusalem get CWS support. The director of this YWCA is Doris Salah, a Latin Rite Catholic who was born in Jerusalem. She took the post in 1966, after working as a guide in the Jordan pavilion of the 1964–65 New York World's Fair.

She directs a program that includes kindergartens in refugee camps, vocational training in Jericho, activities of a women's group, summer camps and regular YWCA activities in the building in Jerusalem. A fervent nationalist who speaks of Palestine as an existing entity, she fosters Palestinian cultural activity through a "Know Your Country" program. She also serves as a member of the Vatican Justice and Peace Commission's local unit in Jerusalem.

In November 1979, another consultation on Palestinian refugees was held in Nicosia. It was called by the Middle East Council in cooperation with CICARWS. In a "Message of the Consultation to the Churches," participants urged churches and other groups to "extend and intensify their material and moral support" of Palestinian refugees.

Meeting shortly after the consultation, the CWS Committee urged member denominations to increase their Service Department support from $250,000 in 1979 to $350,000 in 1980, when the Department's total budget was projected to reach $1.6 million.

The consultation supported the right of Palestinians to "statehood in Palestine, along with existing states in the region," and called on the churches to "promote the idea that the PLO must be admitted as full partner into any deliberations dealing with the future of Palestine." But in a new departure for Palestinians, it recognized that even establishment of a state would not solve the total refugee problem, since any foreseeable state would be too small to accommodate all Palestinians. So the consultation urged "regional cooperation, characterized by mutual acceptance and accommodation between Muslims, Christians and Jews."

Beginning in 1977, CWS issued appeals totalling $600,000 for Lebanon, and most of that was received within two years. Part of the money went to repair church institutions such as schools and hospitals that were damaged in the 1975-78 communal strife. Some went to a village development project that helped people stay in their villages, rather than flock to Beirut and create further congestion and social problems.

These funds also aided a school the Middle East Council set up in an abandoned restaurant on the beach outside South Beirut to serve children to a predominantly Muslim community. They had been driven out of Karantina, a Beirut area, by "Christian" attacks, and so took temporary refuge in beach cabanas.

The Middle East Council had first set up an ad hoc committee to deal with the Lebanese crisis. But in January 1977 it established a Committee for Emergency Relief and Reconstruction to carry out a longer range program. It appointed a Lebanese economist, Iskander Mekarbel, to serve as director. The committee was instructed to assit war victims "regardless of their religious or ideological affiliation." And it subsequently distributed food and blankets to people in all the contending groups.

Gabi Habib and the Middle East Council also sought to fill a mediating role among the opposed forces, and to help outsiders better understand what was happening. In the outside world, news accounts commonly reported the conflict as a war of Christians against Muslims or against Muslim Palestinians, not recognizing that many Palestinians, including some of the leadership, were Christian.

The Council interpreted the conflict as a political and economic struggle with religious overtones, and did not support the "Christian" side. Lebanon's political structure had been based on power sharing among religious communities, with the Maronite Catholics dominant. Only a Maronite could become president and only a Maronite could head the army. Adding to the mix, this arrangement reinforced a dominant economic position held by the Maronite community. The Maronites and another, smaller Eastern Rite Catholic group, the Melkites, were not members of the Council. But Mr. Habib maintained personal contacts among all groups and kept up an effort to bring about a peaceful resolution of the struggle, though without notable success. The judgment that the conflict was not religious gained further validation from the Maronite patriarch's refusal to endorse the efforts of soldiers fighting under the Christian banner.

Though most CWS aid to the Middle East goes to the Council of Churches and Palestinian refugee work, some other programs are supported. In Egypt, these include the work of Samuel Habib (no relation to Gabriel), who is stated clerk of the Coptic Evangelical Church, a product of Presbyterian mission work. He grew up in an Evangelical family and has become one of the outstanding church leaders of the younger generation.

In addition to his work as stated clerk, he directs the Coptic Evangelical Organization for Social Services (CEOSS). This agency conducts a program of village work that has now reached more than 70 villages of Upper Egypt. It began with literacy work, so people could read the Bible. From that it went into publishing of other Christian literature, and then into general community development.

An outstanding younger leader of the Coptic Orthodox Church is Bishop Athanasius of Beni-Suef. A shy, soft-spoken man, he has identified himself closely with the needs of his people and gained a position of respect among Protestants and Muslims, as well as his fellow Orthodox. When he and Samuel Habib visited the United States in 1977, an old woman from Beni-Suef came up at a meeting in Chicago and asked the bishop if he still had the red carpet. She recalled from her youth that whenever the bishop of that era left his house, servants rolled out a red carpet for him to walk on. But Bishop Athanasius was so far removed from such a conception of his role that he had no idea what she was talking about.

A primary interest of Bishop Athanasius has been helping his people build better housing. In the past they normally made their houses of mud bricks. But since construction of the Aswan Dam, new topsoil was not coming down in such great quantities as in the past. So continuing to make mud bricks would deplenish the soil needed for crops. To offset this problem, Bishop Athanasius got the people to using stone, changing a tradition of 5000 years. And CWS has given funds to help purchase stone cutting equipment for this program.

Another program that receives American support is an effort by the Coptic Orthodox Church to aid garbage collectors in Cairo. They live in communities in the garbage disposal areas and build their houses of scrap wood and metal that they salvage. Since garbage is fed to pigs and observant Muslims have nothing to do with pigs, garbage collecting in Egypt has traditionally been a Christian occupation, with jobs passed along generation to generation by family inheritance.

Coptic Pope Shenouda III has a Bishopric for Social and Ecumenical Services that conducts the program for garbage collectors. It is headed by Bishop Samuel, a key ecumenical figure who serves as one of three presidents of the Middle East Council, a vice president of the All Africa Conference of Churches and a member of the World Council's Central Committee.

Under his jurisdiction, the program for garbage collectors is directed by a Coptic Orthodox layman, Yohnna el Ragheb. In "Hope for Life," a film on Middle East churches produced for use in the 1979 Middle East mission study, he is heard explaining that these *zebalein* (collectors of garbage and trash) live in five settlements around Cairo and enjoy little contact with the rest of society. "They feel as if they're lost," he says. The program of the Coptic Church encourages them to build their houses in areas separated from the garbage, and to maintain better sanitation.

It seeks to make their work more remunerative by introducing technology they can use in recycling trash, such as paper. And it offers training in carpentry, metal work and other trades for young men of the community so they will have a choice about their future and not necessarily be forced to following an inherited occupation.

The Turkish invasion of Cyprus in 1974, and the occupation of the northern part of the island, left 200,000 Greek Cypriots displaced. The (Greek) Church of Cyprus operated a Cyprus Refugee Service Program in cooperation with the World Council of Churches and with some support from CWS. It provides three-year loans without interest to small businesses for expansion purposes. It also gives scholarships to high school students and supports other youth programs.

In the period immediately after the displacement, when people were still living in tents, recreation programs were important not only for youth but also for adult men. Their farms and businesses were lost and for a time they had little to do. So their frustrations could easily lead them to start fighting among themselves or engaging in other disruptive activities. So the churches served by organizing athletic teams and providing equipment.

The International YWCA, in cooperation with the YWCA of Greece, sent a Belgian social worker with experience helping Greek migrant workers and some knowledge of the language, Christine Navett, to work with the displaced women of Cyprus. Given the cultural traditions, women could not go to the coffee houses, so they had no place. To meet the need for some activity to fill their empty hours, a separate tent was set up for them and provided with books, handicraft materials and other attractions. Ms. Navett later went on to another assignment, but as a result of her work, Cyprus now has a YWCA.

In Turkey, CWS faced a situation different from most other parts of the Middle East. The country has virtually no Christians except among the minority Armenian, Greek and Syrian communities. So American churches could find no church agency that would serve as an effective vehicle for reaching the majority Turkish population. But they found a private agency that could fill the role.

CWS has established a relationship with the Development Foundation of Turkey (DFT), an agency founded and headed by Altan Unver. Born a Muslim, Mr. Unver attended Tarsus College, which is operated, in the Apostle Paul's native city, by the United Church of

Christ's Near East Mission. He then attended Robert College in Istanbul, which was formerly a mission school. Subsequently, he came to the United States, where he studied engineering and business administration. He also got involved in Quaker work camps.

Back in Turkey, Mr. Unver got a job teaching at Tarsus College. He and his wife began opening their home to students attending a government high school in Tarsus, many of whom were a long way from their native villages.

With a growing concern for the problems of people in these villages, he began organizing weekend work camps that took college students out to the villages so they would develop a better understanding of life there, and perhaps come to feel a responsibility for helping the villagers improve their lives.

When a project to start villagers in poultry raising initially failed because the day-old chicks he distributed all died, he realized that technical knowledge would be required for any successful development program. So he organized the DFT.

In 1977, CWS joined with British, Danish, German and Swiss church agencies in a consortium under the World Council umbrella to support Mr. Unver in the work of his new foundation. They pledged to give a total of $400,000 a year from 1977 to 1979, with $150,000 a year of that amount coming from the United States. At the end of this period, when the DFT had attracted government and World Bank funding, American aid was reduced to $70,000 for 1980. As in many other cases, CWS saw its role not in a continuing program but in temporary support to help a pioneering project demonstrate its worth.

To assist the DFT in evaluation and planning, an American Episcopalian, Lucy Richardson, was sent to serve on the headquarters staff. She had a special interest in the role of women, so in addition to her regular staff work, she worked with women to develop a carpet weaving project to help them gain a better quality of life by learning new skills and marketing their woven products.

The project began in the east Turkey town of Diyarbakir. The DFT was helping people of the surrounding villages improve their livestock, so relationships with the people of the area had already been established.

The carpet weaving project was uniquely suited to the needs of the women and to their culture. It was really a matter of reviving an art that had been in decline for the past few years, so it was a way to reclaim a part of the culture which was both creative and economically productive. In addition, the women could work in their homes, an

Seedlings for the reafforestation program in Algeria.

important factor in that area.

DFT obtained looms, patterns and wool yarn from a government handicrafts program and opened a training center to teach weaving to young women. While Miss Richardson was the catalyst who helped bring the project into being, the project continues today under the momentum of the women themselves.

In Algeria, CWS supported a program of relief and reconstruction carried out by a World Council of Churches consortium, the Christian Committee for Service in Algeria (CCSA), after the war for independence. A major aspect of this effort was a reafforestation program that involved the planting of 40 million trees—not for lumber but to help control soil and surface water on the hillsides of eastern Algeria.

The program began in 1962 with a three-year plan. But the CCSA did not go in with the idea of establishing a permanent institution. Rather, it wanted to get the work started and then turn it over to the Algerians.

So the second three-year period, 1965–68, was one of transition, with a semi-autonomous government agency taking responsibility for the program, and the CCSA continuing to serve the country for a time as a sort of talent brokerage agency, bringing in various specialists.

A Swiss director got the program started, and then it was taken over by Hans Aurbakken, a native of Norway who had served in Algeria since 1938 under the U.S. Methodist Church and later served on the New York staff of the United Methodist Board of Global Ministries, World Division.

"We had twenty churches and church organizations involved and twelve nationalities on our staff," he says. "The reafforestation program represented more than half our budget, but we also had social-educational and medical-health programs integrated into the total operation."

CWS secured Food for Peace commodities that were distributed to Algerian workers on a food-for-work basis. "We always got workers from the local communities where we were planting trees," Mr. Aurbakken says. "So they became interested and later protected the saplings. Because they had become personally involved in the project, they would keep their goats out and so on."

Today the contribution of the churches to this project has been completed. But every year, Algeria still holds a tree planting day to continue the work that they began.

7

Ireland
Peace—Justice—Reconciliation

The concern for reconciliation that plays a role in almost every CWS effort, has been even more central in its Ireland program. This program has not been directed to a nation suffering from the extreme poverty of the Third World, though its economic problems are serious, or to a nation suffering from a natural disaster. But it has been directed to a nation suffering nonetheless. The conflict over the governance of Northern Ireland, or Ulster, brought not only many deaths and injuries, but also terror, fear, hatred and despair.

CWS became involved in part because the tragedy had a religious dimension. The conflict set two communities with their separate cultures and histories against each other. But these two communities were identified with two expressions of the Christian faith—Roman Catholic and Protestant. This made it a scandal throughout the world, for people everywhere read of Catholic and Protestant Christians hating and killing each other.

Another reason for the involvement of an American church agency was the need to help Americans of Irish descent better understand the conflict. Not only are many American Catholics of Irish background, but many Protestants also trace their ancestry to the Protestant communities of Ireland. The largest Protestant church in Ireland is Presbyterian, a sister to Presbyterian churches of the United States. The Episcopal and United Methodist Churches also have counterparts there.

Consequently, many Americans have been caught up in the emotions of the Irish conflict. And they have been involved in various campaigns waged in the United States on behalf of Irish groups. The

Irish conflict has become a controversial political issue in the United States, and prominent Irish-American politicians have felt impelled to take a stand on questions about how the conflict should be pursued and resolved.

The Ireland program began with requests from the Irish Council of Churches for assistance with some of the peace projects it was sponsoring. CWS decided that involvement in Ireland would be appropriate, and appealed for funds to support an Ireland program.

In July 1975, David Bowman, a Jesuit priest whose forebears came from Ireland's County Limerick, now part of the Republic of Ireland, was employed as a full time staff member for this program, administratively located in the Europe and Middle East Department with Richard Butler.

Father Bowman served until November 1979, when he took a position in Washington, D.C., as secretary for ministries of the national Jesuit Conference. Even after that, however, he was retained by the Division of Overseas Ministries on a part time consultancy basis to maintain contact with Ireland.

Father Bowman first came to the National Council of Churches in 1966 from a teaching post at the Catholic University of America in Washington, D.C. The Council employed him to help it develop some of the new relationships with the Catholic Church that became possible following Vatican II.

The first Catholic ever employed on the Council's professional staff, he assisted a joint task force that explored the question of Catholic membership in the Council. This task force had a membership of top level officials from both sides, and after careful study it issued a report that, although refraining from offering any specific recommendation, said no reason existed to keep the Catholic Church of the United States from joining the National Council of Churches.

Several Catholic dioceses took up the question and made favorable decisions, but then the church's national leadership apparently decided that they were not ready to make an application. So the question dropped from discussion. Father Bowman then began working with the National Council's Commission on Regional and Local Ecumenism, an appropriate slot since the regional and local ecumenical units were where Catholics were getting involved. Numerous Catholic dioceses joined state councils or conferences of churches, and the membership of Catholic parishes in local councils was becoming common throughout the country.

But meanwhile the Irish situation was worsening. In 1969 began

This burned out area in Belfast grimly depicts the threat of violence which is a daily threat to the people of northern Ireland.

what were called "the troubles," with an increase in violence, subsequent breakdown of government authority in Ulster and then direct rule from London. Lines of division were hardening, and assassins ruling by terror. Father Bowman felt a deep concern about this situation, and began looking for ways that Americans might be helpful.

In January 1972, he went with Donald Campion, editor of the Jesuit magazine, *America,* and Wesley Baker, a minister in the United Presbyterian ecumenical office, to visit both Northern Ireland and the Republic of Ireland. After many conversations with clergy, government officials and other people on all sides of the conflict, they concluded that the Irish people would welcome outside help, and that there were some things Americans could do.

Father Bowman and Mr. Baker subsequently led in organizing a group of interested people who called themselves Colleagues from American Churches. They raised funds for Irish projects, coordinated the sending of American volunteers for summer work with Irish children and other programs and maintained a network of communication. In connection with one of his responsibilities in the Jesuit order, Father Bowman was attending regular meetings in Europe, and he could use these trips as occasions for making side visits to Ireland.

When funds became available for an Ireland program staff member, Father Bowman stood out as the logical choice, both because of his deep interest and accumulated experience and because of the ecumenical dimension he added. The idea of a Protestant and Orthodox organization employing a Roman Catholic priest to carry out its Ireland program in itself made a strong witness.

Father Bowman had been serving as president of Colleagues, and he gave up that office when he took the new position. But he kept in close contact, and again became president when he ended his period of full time service with CWS.

The Ireland program objectives were to:

—sensitize the American churches to what was happening in Ireland.

—take U.S. church leaders on visits to Ireland in search of deeper understanding.

—offer resources for the use of Irish churches, helping them in their task of serving as agents of reconciliation.

—assist centers such as Corrymeela in their work for peace.

—provide authentic interpretation to the American churches about developments in Ireland.

As part of his work, Father Bowman continued to visit Ireland regularly, and maintained an extensive network of contacts among both Catholics and Protestant in North and South.

In 1976, he arranged for a large American delegation to visit Ireland and participate in a rally sponsored by the Peace People at the Boyne, where the Protestant William of Orange defeated the Catholic James II in 1690.

This was an event that still stood out in the mind of Father Bowman's secretary, Liddy Paterson, when she wrote a farewell note in the Ireland program bulletin in 1979:

"I have been with the Ireland program for 3¾ years and the time has really flown by. There are so many wonderful memories that will remain with me. I will always remember the Journey of Reconciliation in 1976 in which I participated with 110 Americans. We visited Dublin, Belfast and L-Derry. We met church leaders and community leaders from both communities who spoke to us in depth about their arduous work towards peace and reconciliation in Northern Ireland. It was so exhilarating to meet some of the people and projects which the NCC Ireland program has funded; e.g., Glencree in the Republic of Ireland, Corrymeela and Peace Point, Belfast. To see this first hand was a profoundly moving experience for me, and also made me acutely aware of the complexities of the problems in Northern Ireland. It was also fascinating to witness Fr. Bowman's very effective diplomacy in the North and the Republic, and to meet many of the people who visit us over here.

"I stayed with the Ingram family in Lisburn, N.I., and later helped Stephanie come over to live with the Patricia Kennedy Lawford family in New York for a year—a Presbyterian teenager from the working class, in a Catholic home. It worked out wonderfully well, and Stephanie stays in touch with her friends and us."

Another example of Father Bowman's work was sponsoring a week-long information seminar in June 1978 for 35 church and media representatives. It was held in Belfast and offered exposure to all sides of the conflict.

To strengthen the ecumenical witness of the American churches, the Ireland program gave funds to Irish projects through an Interchurch Emergency Fund. This agency was set up jointly by the Irish Catholic Church and the Irish Council of Churches.

Another dimension of the Ireland program was joining with the Catholic peace agency, Pax Christi-USA, to raise funds ecumenically in the United States for ecumenical use in Ireland.

Still another part of Father Bowman's work was helping arrange for the visit of people from the Irish churches and peace groups to the United States. He helped them plan their itineraries so they could meet with individuals particularly interested in learning about the Irish situation, speak to church and other meetings and present their experience through the news media.

He developed a close working relationship with Canon William Arlow, whose service from 1975 to the end of 1979 as secretary of the Irish Council of Churches, almost exactly coincided with Father Bowman's own full time service in the Ireland program.

Shortly before joining CWS, Father Bowman worked through Colleagues to arrange a three-week visit for two Irish lay people— Sean Cooney, a Catholic, and Anne Sloan, an Anglican.

One day in March 1975 they held a press conference in New York, and toward the end a reporter from one of the local dailies expressed surprise. "I thought my editor was sending me to report on a debate between a Catholic and a Protestant," he said.

But what he heard was something quite different. Mr. Cooney and Mrs. Sloan were not opposing each other as Catholic against Protestant, but were standing together as people of peace against the people of violence. And in connection with this emphasis, they were urging people everywhere they went in the United States to exercise caution in contributing money for use in Ireland. Many sympathetic Americans, particularly among Irish Catholics whose emotions were still atuned to the Republic's struggle for independence from England, were giving out of a desire to help their suffering cousins in the Six Counties. But sometimes the money seemed to wind up causing new suffering.

So people who came to hear Mr. Cooney and Mrs. Sloan found them making such statements as:

"Fund raising in the U.S.A. for women and children in need is perfectly all right, but there are no starving children in Ireland, despite the rhetoric of some who raise money on that basis. The welfare is high enough, and goes to families of men in Long Kesh [prison] too. Check where your money goes; check this again and again, for some men and women lie dead in our cemeteries due to bombs and bullets bought with American money. We've received not a penny from such collections for community development, nor did we in '69 or '71 when we suffered so much. Where does that money go? We never see a bit of it, though we need it for improving the quality of life in our areas."

That message was not heard gladly in all quarters. In Chicago,

Martin McGing of the Northern Aid Committee, a group assisting Catholics in Northern Ireland, wrote in *The Irish People:*

"Ironically those two people came here presumably as delegates to a church council or Council of Churches, and they came here with a message which in reality would amount to a genocide of a large part of the population of the Six Counties, in their best Hitler fashion. Of course, Oliver Cromwell also preached religion and in the name of religion murdered the women, the children of Drogheda and other cities in Ireland."

Such rhetoric showed the need for American churches to conduct an Ireland program. A key objective was to provide a reliable channel of funds for people who wanted to give with some assurance that their money would really be used to help and not to finance more violence.

The theme of the Ireland program was "justice-peace-reconciliation." Peace was the central concern, but no peace was possible without justice. So the Ireland program supported projects that kept both peace and justice in view, and people who worked for the final goal of reconciliation.

During the period Father Bowman was full time with the program, it collected $118,000 for support of projects in Ireland. The largest amount from this fund, $35,000, went to finance work of the Irish Council of Churches. The next largest $30,000 went to Belfast Peace Point, an agency directed by Mr. Cooney.

But a great many other projects received support, often small amounts but grants that served to encourage beleaguered people and to reassure them that they were not alone. They were part of an international Christian community that expressed its concern for them.

Starting in march 1977, David Stevens, projects director for the Irish Council of Churches, provided a valuable service for the Ireland program by accepting applications for grants, making recommendations for action on them and then evaluating results.

Dr. Stevens noted, "Many small local self-starting projects were helped. Some of these are now fully supported from statutory sources or have become viable projects in their own right. Others unfortunately found things too difficult and have not survived.

"We have helped a considerable number of church or church-oriented bodies relate to the situation better in Northern Ireland, e.g. Ulster Quaker Service Committee, Shankill Team Ministry, Shankill Employment Project, Holy Trinity Family Care Centre. I feel that this has been particularly important and beneficial."

In a concluding word, Dr. Stevens said: "The Ireland Programme Fund has been valuable in the support of a wide range of projects in the peace-justice-reconciliation, voluntary, church, inter-church and community self-help fields. It has been able to offer tangible support to many different people working in many different fields for a better community during a time of much violence and tension. These people have many times expressed their gratitude to me and it is right at this moment that this gratitude should be more directly expressed by me on their behalf to the National Council of Churches in the USA."

The type of activity that people involved with the Ireland program thought best contributed to justice-peace-reconciliation was illustrated by the two lay visitors Father Bowman had brought to the United States.

Mr. Cooney served as president and Mrs. Sloan as vice-president of the North Belfast Community Council, which included 60 organizations working in community development. Mr. Cooney had also organized the Crumlin Construction Company, an ecumenical operation to rebuild burned out houses in the Ardoyne area of North Belfast. This had been a mixed Catholic-Protestant area, and he was concerned to see it rebuilt as a sign of the possibility that Catholics and Protestants could live together.

A small, wiry man of working class manner and speech, Mr. Cooney maintained contacts in many corners of Irish society. He had six nephews in Long Kesh Prison at one time, three on life terms, and visited there often. He talked with representatives of the Irish Republican Army (IRA) and the Protestant Ulster Defense Association. But he contended that the only way forward was by building a better life for all people on the local community level.

Mrs. Sloan and her husband made their living operating a postal station and a small store, but devoted much of their time to community work. A building known as the Community Shop served as their base of operations.

"The Irish do not want more Americans coming over to do sociological surveys on them or to gather material for doctoral dissertations," Father Bowman observed. "But they feel a sense of isolation, and they are appreciative when outside churches show concern."

"There is no doubt that we have credibility," he said. "They approve of what we do and want us to continue. We have no program of our own, but only seek to help the people there with their programs, working on their terms. We have made no initiatives except to visit

71

them and ask if there was anything we could do."

"I am not dealing with the conflict," he said, "but with people caught in the conflict. And I am offering service on their terms."

"Obviously, my favored position stems largely from my being a Jesuit priest in the employ of the NCC," he said. "Once the Irish get used to the paradox, they usually like it."

Among Father Bowman's activities was issuing an occasional bulletin, which was circulated to people interested in the Ireland program. In this bulletin he reported on his own activities, including his frequent visits to Northern Ireland and the Republic, and on what key individuals and groups involved with the Irish situation were saying and doing.

In these bulletins he expressed his own strong opposition to violence: "Violence prevents steps toward justice and peace; murder is murder and not 'political execution;' political injustice is the occasion and excuse for violence; all violence, 'legal' and illegal, must stop. Only then can political change occur."

The July 1979 Bulletin reported on leadership development programs that would bring Irish teenagers to Wilmington Delaware, and Lake Charles, Louisiana:

"As readers of this Bulletin know, we favor funding holidays for Irish children in *Ireland* or *Northern* Ireland, rather than spending thousands of dollars on transportation in the USA. These leadership programs for teenagers, however, seem to us to be a good use of money, since they are planned carefully and are not just 'holidays for children.' "

This issue of the Bulletin also reported that volunteers were continuing to go to Ireland and staff summer programs. In the summer of 1979, 13 were going to work in the Ardoyne, 8 to Corrymeela and others to Lurgan, Portadown and Glencree.

Even more acutely than some other situations, Ireland forced CWS to consider its limitations. It was convinced that Americans had a role to play in Ireland, and that the American churches should demonstrate their concern. But it likewise recognized that the primary responsibility remained with the people of Ireland. They were the ones who would provide the answers to the agony of their conflict if any were to be had. Americans could support them, and could avoid some actions that would make the situation worse, but the American role could never be more than supplementary.

In all areas, CWS has to acknowledge that its resources are limited, and it cannot pretend to solve all problems. Deciding what an outside agency can do that is helpful in a situation such as the Irish conflict is not easy. A starting point is consultation with church leaders and other people involved in the situation. CWS listened to the people of Ireland, and got their suggestions about ways an outside body might assist them. They encouraged American church involvement, and expressed gratitude for the concern that was shown.

The Ireland program also raises the question of how long the churches should continue in one area. They cannot maintain permanent programs for all areas of the world. Yet, the basic situations of need often continue over decades. How does a church agency define specific objectives, carry out programs to meet those objectives and then terminate its operation?

8

Refugees
The 80's—A Decade of Refugees

A poet of ancient Israel wrote words that express the assurance needed by those who are separated from their homeland and bereft of all that is familiar and dear. It could be called the Psalm of the Refugee:

> I lift up my eyes to the hills.
> From whence does my help come?
> My help comes from the Lord,
>   who made heaven and earth.
>
> He will not let your foot be moved,
>   he who keeps you will not slumber.
> Behold, he who keeps Israel
>   will neither slumber nor sleep.
>
> The Lord is your keeper;
>   the Lord is your shade
>   on your right hand.
> The sun shall not smite you by day,
>   nor the moon by night.
>
> The Lord will keep you from all evil;
>   he will keep your life.
> The Lord will keep
>   your going out and your coming in
>   from this time forth and for evermore.
>   Psalm 121

Natural calamities and human-created disasters continue to uproot people.

The refugee's deepest desire is to go home. When that is impossible, the desire is to find a new home. In either case, CWS stands ready to help.

Its staff spends more time on aiding refugees than on any other single task. And refugee aid has been central to its work from the first. The end of World War II left millions of people adrift or temporarily housed in displaced persons camps. Many of these were people from areas of Eastern Europe that had come under communist rule, and they were unable or unwilling to return. The American churches moved to help the displaced get resettled in their own or other nearby countries where that was feasible, and in other cases to help them take up a new life in America.

At the beginning, refugee resettlement seemed like a temporary, post-war task. After the displacements resulting from World War II were rectified, presumably this would no longer present a problem.

But new refugee situations continually develop, and when the first Pan-African Conference on Refugees convened in Addis Ababa in 1967, the continent had an estimated one million refugees. When the second Pan-African Conference on Refugees was held in Arusha, Tanzania in 1979, the estimate was four million.

At the same time, the United Nations High Commissioner for Refugees was estimating that the number worldwide was 14 million. The twentieth century has turned into the century of homeless people.

The biblical accounts of Jacob and his family going to Egypt to escape famine and of Joseph and Mary taking Jesus to Egypt to escape the tyranny of Herod illustrate the two primary forces that have continued to create refugees throughout history—economic distress and political oppression.

American Christians recognize a special responsibility to the refugee from both their "American" and their "Christian" perspectives. As Christians, they remember that their Lord was once a refugee, and they are serving him whenever they serve those who flee oppression. "I was a stranger and you welcomed me" (Matt. 25:35). As Americans, they recognize that they live in a nation created by economic and political refugees. Even the Indians were once immigrants looking for a new home.

Through the centuries of American history, it has been part of the national purpose to offer refuge to people seeking liberty and enlarged opportunity. At times this purpose was upheld more strongly than at others, but it has always remained part of the American heritage. The

Statue of Liberty stands holding her torch aloft in New York harbor to symbolize this role.

In its various programs, CWS serves four kinds of refugees. First are people who fled their country and are returning to it. Many Africans fall in this category. CWS helped Angolans return after their country won its independence from Portugal, and many Ugandans after the overthrow of Idi Amin. It has also helped some Latin Americans, such as Argentinians returning home after the death of Juan Peron.

Second are people resettled from one part of a country to another part. Indonesia has been a key example in this category. People were taken from an area considered over-populated to a less populated area. CWS, working through the Indonesian Council of Churches, helped them get reestablished in their new homes. Coming under this category in a sense are Greek Cypriots, who were forced from their homes by the Turkish invasion. Some Turkish Cypriots, too, were displaced and were offered help, but the Turkish government did not accept it.

Third are people moving from their country to another country, but not to the United States. CWS has helped refugees such as Angolans settling in Zaire and Palestinians settling in Latin America. During the Sudan War, it helped 500,000 Sudanese resettle in five other countries of the area. Recently it has helped Eritrean refugees resettle in the Sudan.

When the Dalai Lama came to the United States in 1979, the first time any Dalai Lama had traveled to the Western hemisphere, his itinerary included a visit to the Interchurch Center in New York. He went to the CWS offices there to express his thanks for the help he and his people had received since they left Tibet in 1959 to take refuge in India.

The refugee program of the World Council of Churches assists many refugees in this category, and CWS serves as a channel for American churches contributing to the World Council program. It also helps national councils and other colleague agencies that aid refugees. An example is the Hong Kong Christian Council's Division of Christian Service, which aids Chinese and Vietnamese refugees coming there.

A fourth category of refugees are those who are resettled in the United States. These include both refugees who come under government auspices and those who come seeking asylum without government clearance. The latter are commonly called "illegal aliens," but people working in church resettlement efforts prefer the term "undocumented" to indicate that their presence in the United

When the Dalai Lama made his first visit in 25 years to the U.S., he called on Church World Service to express appreciation for aid to Tibetan refugees. Left to right: His Holiness, the Dalai Lama, his interpreter, the author.
(UMC Board of Global Ministries photo)

States is often justified even if they haven't secured all the proper legal documents. Of this group, most CWS attention has gone to the Haitians arriving in Florida by boat.

Over its total history, CWS has helped resettle some 250,000 refugees in the United States. In recent years the largest number have been Indochinese. Previously, the largest group were the Cubans who were resettled after the Revolution led by Fidel Castro.

CWS assisted a number of Hungarian refugees resettle in the United States after Soviet troops put down the uprising of 1956. And it has resettled refugees from other Eastern European countries, members of minority groups such as the Kurds from the Middle East, Uganda Asians expelled by Idi Amin and many others.

From one perspective, helping refugees seems among the least debatable activities a church agency could carry out. When suffering and oppressed people seek refuge, most everyone would agree, a Christian service agency ought to assist.

Yet, refugee work does arouse debate. Some observers have asked whether the churches were sometimes giving people too much encouragement to solve their problems by emigrating to the United States. This question was raised, for example, in connection with the massive resettlement program for Cubans.

Nancy Nicalo, who has served as director of the CWS refugee office since 1977, replies, "If we are good at our work of resettlement, perhaps we encourage some others to become refugees. But that is a small part of the situation. The risks for a refugee are so great that it takes a deeper motivation."

Other questions revolve around relationships with government in refugee resettlement. The U.S. government relies on voluntary agencies to handle the actual work of finding sponsors for refugees and assisting the refugees to get settled in their new homes.

CWS itself has raised questions about U.S. policies that grant refugee status to people fleeing communist oppression but not people fleeing the oppression of right wing governments such as Haiti or Chile. The American public often seems much more willing to aid people escaping from communist governments than those escaping other oppressive regimes, especially when the U.S. government is allied with those regimes. How closely do the churches want to become identified with the government in implementing its refugee policies?

The case of the Haitians was especially instructive because they risked the dangers of escape in frail boats as the Vietnamese were doing about the same time. But though the U.S. government made

79

special efforts to help the Vietnamese boat people, it put Haitian boat people in jail, denied them work permits and moved to deport them. The churches interceded on behalf of the Haitians, recognizing that they faced likely imprisonment and possible death if they were returned to the dictatorship of Haiti's Jean Claude (Baby Doc) Duvalier. More than 2500 Haitians have risked the 800-mile boat trip to Florida since 1972.

Ms. Nicalo says the acceptance of government money for refugee resettlment does not constitute a problem in itself. Without it, she says, CWS would not be able to do nearly as much for the refugees—unless the churches raised much larger sums for this program than they do now, which hardly seems likely.

But she says voluntary agencies do need to remain alert in preserving their independence from government. "Sometimes we become advocates for a case when the government denies admission, or for groups such as the Haitians," she says.

CWS entered into a new relationship with the U.S. State Department in 1977 when it began placing staff members in Malaysia to help with some of the processing that State Department personnel normally perform. "The number of Vietnamese refugees was increasing and the State Department refugee office couldn't get additional staff, so they asked the voluntary agencies for help in documenting the refugees," says Ms. Nicalo. "We somewhat reluctantly agreed that we would place representatives of one agency in each country to represent everybody. Then we looked at who already had relationships in a particular country, and Church World Service was in Malaysia."

Even after the State Department placed personnel in Malaysia for refugee processing, because of the extraordinary pressure of so many refugees waiting in miserable camps there, CWS stayed on to help. At the end of 1979 its staff had grown to include 20 Americans and 40-50 local employees. And it was continuing to assert its independent status and resisting State Department efforts to exercise control of its staff. "We live in cooperative tension," says Ms. Nicalo.

U.S. voluntary organizations engaged in refugee resettlement coordinate their work through the American Council of Voluntary Agencies. A member of the refugee staff attends meetings that are held weekly, or sometimes more often, at the Council's New York headquarters. Agency representatives sitting around the table there decide who will handle which refugees.

CWS also coordinates its work with the World Council of Churches, which has a Refugee Office as part of its Commission on Inter-Church Aid, Refugee and World Service (CICARWS). In addition to the main office in Geneva, it maintains branch offices in Vienna, Athens and Rome. An office was formerly maintained in Beirut but was closed during the fighting in Lebanon. Subsequently, Middle East refugees who had been served by the Beirut office were referred to the Athens office.

Part of the resettlement program is encouraging local congregations to serve as sponsors and help a refugee or refugee family get started in a new life. This task is handled primarily through the denominational offices. They appeal through denominational channels for congregations willing to serve as sponsors, and then match refugees with sponsors.

Sponsorship responsibilities include locating housing, providing enough food, furniture and general household supplies to give refugees a start and assisting with job hunting. Sponsors also help with such problems as getting children enrolled in schools.

Usually, a smaller group within a congregation first gets interested in serving as a sponsor, but gradually the whole congregation tends to get involved. Resettlement agencies like to have a group rather than an individual or one family serve as sponsor because a group can call on larger and more varied resources if the refugees have special needs, and can continue to function if a key individual has to drop out.

CWS serves sponsors and denominational offices as a backup agency, offering assistance and counsel when refugees have extraordinary medical and legal problems, or experience other difficulties in adjusting. In 1979, it took some of the money it received from the government for refugee resettlement and began using it to help local councils of churches employ staff for refugee work. These staff members enlist refugee sponsors and provide services such as language classes for refugees who do not know English.

Most refugees soon become self-supporting. But as with any group of people, some run into unavoidable difficulty and need more help. There may be a death in the family. If the breadwinner dies or becomes incapacitated, the family may be forced to turn to some outside source of help. In some cases, such as the Cuban and Indochina resettlement programs, Congress has made provision for refugees to get welfare assistance in case of necessity. But other refugees are excluded from such benefits. So if they run into difficulty, the agencies that handled their resettlement will need to provide the extra resources that are needed. In a few cases, where refugees experience certain medical or mental disabilities, they may need assistance for the rest of their lives. "Love," the Apostle Paul wrote, "never ends" (1 Cor. 13:8).

Resettlement of refugees is a more complicated process than just sending a telegram that says, "Come on. We'll meet you at the plane." To illustrate, take a family of Kampuchean refugees, the Kims.

On May 10, 1979, Peng Nhan Kim fled to Thailand with his wife, three daughters, two sons and a brother-in-law. The government of Thailand placed them in a camp for refugees, Buriran, and they then came under the authority of the United Nations High Commissioner for Refugees.

Through UN arrangements, representatives of resettlement agencies in various countries were visiting the camps to interview refugees. So the Kims were able to express some choice about where they wished to resettle. They had an uncle aleady resettled in the United States, and this made the United States a logical destination for them.

The American agencies had designated the International Rescue Committee to represent them all in Thailand. It operated a Joint Voluntary Agency Office there, and used interview forms the agencies had all agreed upon.

On June 26, a case worker employed by the International Rescue Committee visited Buriran, and the Kims came to apply for resettlement in the United States. The case worker interviewed them, and filled out forms giving information about ages, education, vocational skills and so on.

Mr. Kim, 39 years old, was a nurse but, like most refugees, said he would take any kind of employment he might be offered. His wife had no specific skills, but also agreed to take any kind of work. The interviewer noted that she was four months pregnant, which would affect not only her future employment prospects but also travel and perhaps other aspects of her resettlement.

The Kims were case number 31,699 for the Thailand operation. And their data sheet had "New Khmer" stamped in red, an indication that they were part of a new refugee group that Thailand felt it could not accommodate and would have to send back if they were not quickly resettled elsewhere. So agencies were trying to rush these cases.

In the rush, agencies were sometimes tripping each other up. An American agency might complete all the preparatory work for resettling a family, and then find they had accepted an offer of resettlement in Germany, Australia or some other country. So procedures for better coordination were under discussion as the regular program moved along.

Vietnamese refugee family undergoing interview process at camp at Pulau Bidong, Malaysia.
(UN/Isaac)

No such problem developed with the Kims, but the process still had a long way to go. The Joint Voluntary Agency Office in Thailand sent its interview sheets in a packet with others to the American Council of Voluntary Agencies in New York. And there, in the regular distribution process, it was agreed that CWS would take the Kims.

The next step was approaching the denominational resettlement offices. CWS represents all the 31 National Council of Churches denominations, and a dozen of these maintain active, regular resettlement programs. In addition, two denominations that are not National Council members, the Christian Reformed Church and the Southern Baptist Convention, operate refugee resettlement programs through CWS. The Southern Baptist Home Mission Board, the denomination's resettlement agency, was formerly related through the Baptist World Alliance, but in recent years has maintained a direct relationship. Still another agency working through CWS is the International Division of the YMCA.

CWS staff stay in touch with denominational offices to keep informed about which one is ready to take how many more cases, and what type of cases it might handle most expeditiously. Sometimes sponsors are hard to find; sometimes national publicity about a refugee situation will bring more sponsors than can be used at the moment.

The Kims were assigned to Isis Brown, refugee officer of the Episcopal Church, and she accepted the responsibility of finding a sponsor for them. This turned out to be an interfaith group at Croton-on-Hudson, New York.

While the voluntary agencies were moving their processes forward, the United States government had its legal processes going. A State Department official in Thailand interviewed the Kims to check for security risk and the like. And the Immigration and Naturalization Service (INS) made the final decision that they could be admitted to the United States under applicable laws.

When Isis Brown reported that she had a sponsor for the Kims, CWS notified the American Council of Voluntary Agencies, which sent word to the Thailand office. Then for the actual travel, it turned the Kims over to the Inter-Governmental Committee for European Migration (ICEM).

This agency was established by the United States and other governments to handle the movement of displaced people in Europe after World War II. But subsequently its role was expanded to serve refugees anywhere in the world. Among other services, it lends refugees money for travel to their new homelands. Lends, not gives.

The refugees sign promissory notes saying they will repay the money, which then finances the travel of later refugees. The agency handling resettlement serves as the collection agency, so CWS will maintain a continuing relationship with the Kims in receiving their monthly payments for about three years.

The money is returned to ICEM through CICARWS because, from an international standpoint, the CWS refugee program is part of the World Council's global program. The CICARWS Refugee Office also signs the contracts with the U.S. State Department for the refugees resettled by CWS. Under these contracts, worked out with a Geneva office of the State Department, it pays voluntary agencies $500 per refugee for their services in handling the actual resettlement in American communities.

Some debate has arisen about how agencies should dispose of that $500, particularly over whether any or how much should be used for direct assistance to the individual refugee and how much for financing agency efforts to strengthen the total refugee program.

CWS has decided to use some—$110 at the time the Kims arrived, later raised to $120—for a transitional grant to the refugee. The Kim family included eight people, so $880 went to them on arrival. But as a precaution, the check is made out to both the refugee and the sponsor, so they will begin their new relationship by deciding together how best to use this money. In this way, newcomers are protected against the possibility that some slick salesman might too quickly talk them into spending it all on some attractive but less-than-necessary feature of the consumer society.

ICEM sent a telex stating that the Kims would travel on a charter flight to Travis Air Force Base in San Francisco, arriving August 17. Normally the agencies do not know until just a few days ahead just when the refugees will arrive, so they cannot tell the local sponsors. When the time comes, then a flurry of activity ensues, getting things ready.

Here is another reason for seeking a congregation or some other group to serve as sponsor. In some cases where individuals have signed up as sponsors, the refugees have suddenly flown in while the sponsors were away from home for a few days and couldn't be found.

But in the case of the Kims, a CWS staff member met them in San Francisco and got them onto a commercial flight to Kennedy Airport in New York, where another staff member met them and put them in the hands of their sponsors.

The group at Croton-on-Hudson had signed a form pledging to assist the Kims with job hunting, housing and general orientation. This form does not carry legal force and will not subject the signers to any kind of court action. But by signing, sponsors make a strong moral commitment to stand by their new neighbors as they undertake the difficult adjustment to life in a new land.

This often becomes a way for sponsors to learn important things about their own communities. However many years they may have lived there, they perhaps have not seen the community from the perspective of a refugee needing low cost housing and transportation, a job or aid in the various emergencies that arise. Secure, well-established residents may for the first time see their community from the perspective of the vulnerable, and that can stimulate them to undertake other ministries.

Though attention in recent years has centered on Indochina, refugees continue to come from other parts of the world. On January 12, 1979, Mary Meimari-Byatt, director of the CICARWS refugee office in Athens, sent CWS a list of refugees there who had secured preliminary approval from INS if sponsors could be provided. The list included 16 individuals and families with a total of 27 persons from Albania, Bulgaria, Rumania, the Soviet Union, Vietnam and Ethiopia.

Among those from Rumania were John and Mary Culici, who went to Greece on October 19, 1978, on a tourist visa and decided they would not return. They attended a church in Athens, told some people there of their plans and were advised to contact the CICARWS office. They explained that they found Rumanian life oppressive to their religious life, and that they could not support the communist regime.

While awaiting resettlement, they became friends with several people in Athens, and among them were a retired American professor, Sumner Hayward, and his wife, Lucy. They were going to settle in Ohio, and when they returned to the United States in early 1979, they came to the CWS offices to talk about sponsoring the Culicis.

Since Mrs. Culici's father had been a Baptist minister, the American Baptist refugee officer, Matthew R. Giuffrida, looked for a sponsor among Rumanian Baptists in the United States. But when nothing developed along this line, the Haywards became the sponsors and the Culicis arrived on April 18.

An example of the more unusual refugee cases is Girfan Fatkullin, a Muslim who had been born in Russia but was now a citizen of China's Sinkiang region, between Tibet and the Soviet Union. His sister, Ayse, had immigrated to the United States and was living in Nyack,

New York.

She wrote in 1974, at the time she was becoming a citizen, to request assistance for her brother, and CWS contacted the CICARWS office in Hong Kong. Apparently, China was willing to allow some emigration for reuniting families at the time. But the brother was still in China and needed to fill out forms. The sister's limited command of English, combined with the difficulty of getting correspondence to and from the brother in Sinkiang, caused many delays.

But the story eventually reached its happy ending, when on February 28, 1978, Mr. Fatkullin flew from Hong Kong to Seattle, and from there to New York. There, he and his sister, both in their 70s, were reunited.

He reported that he had spent ten years in jail, and that he had been afraid to tell anyone he had a sister in the United States until President Nixon's visit opened a new era in U.S.-China relations.

What kind of person is the refugee? Generally the refugee is a person of inner strength and determination. Some Americans fear the refugee as a potential burden on society. But the churches find that less than five per cent of the refugees they resettle will fail to become self-supporting. People forced out of their homeland generally feel grateful to the nation that gives them a chance to start anew, and they make every effort to prove themselves good citizens.

Churches know that perfection of character cannot be expected of any refugee, no more than it can of any native born citizen, and inevitably some refugees will act in ways that prove disappointing. But experience has shown that the overwhelming majority will become productive, self-sustaining citizens who contribute to their new community.

In their refugee programs, churches of course do not confine themselves to resettling Christians, but often help people of Muslim, Buddhist or other religions, or of none. But in many cases, a refugee family does become part of the local congregation that served as its sponsor, and the presence of this family adds a new dimension of awareness about the nature of the church as an international fellowship.

In some cases, as Americans are working to resettle refugees, people ask whether the American government is doing all it could to alleviate problems that are generating refugees. This question has arisen in connection with the Vietnamese refugees. Visits to Vietnam since the war have convinced CWS officials that many Vietnamese would not feel pressed to flee if the economic conditions of their country were not so harsh. And it has urged the U.S. government to help alleviate these conditions by establishing diplomatic relations with Vietnam, allowing normal trade and assisting Vietnam in the development of its economy.

Nonetheless, CWS thinks that when Vietnamese do become refugees, those questions become secondary for the moment, and the responsibility of American Christians is to give them all possible aid.

It maintains a separation between its judgment on the broader causes of a refugee movement, and what should be done for the individual refugee who becomes a victim of the larger forces at work.

In the case of Nicaraguan refugees, for example, it has helped some who fled to escape the former Anastasio Somoza government and others and fled its successor when he was ousted. Whatever judgments are made about the two governments, it believes the people who become refugees should receive help.

CWS does not encourage people anywhere in the world to become refugees, or tell them that emigration to America or some other country will solve the problems they face in their own country. But after people have become refugees, then it does what it can to help.

While its staff in the Immigration and Refugee Program give full attention to helping refugees start a new life, they know that their colleagues are giving equal attention to the human rights and developmental problems that caused the refugees to become voyagers in search of a new homeland.

Meanwhile, for millions of other refugees life is one of largely unrelieved misery. They are the forgotten people of our world. They will never walk across your lawn to knock on your door. You will most likely never meet them. But they are a reminder to us of our inability to manage our society, our religion, our politics and our hungers with due concern for the welfare of all.

On the other hand, our continuing efforts to help the refugee—in whatever place by whatever cause—is heartening evidence that the healing impulses of compassion and neighborliness are at work among us, nourishing human hopes for peace and freedom.

9

Development and Human Rights

The exhausted laborer pushing a hand plow through barren soil has no politics. Nor have the refugees who leave behind everything they have known to flee they know not where. Yet development and human rights are political issues in our time.

Concern for justice, concern for the afflicted is part of the Biblical heritage of the church. It is at this point—concern for the victims and for the oppressed—that the churches become involved with development and with human rights.

The efforts of CWS in development, notably agricultural improvement and technical training, but including literacy, nutrition, health care and other programs were brought together in 1977 to establish a development office. Through this office the many aspects of development and the several types of projects in this effort can be coordinated for more effective and purposeful programs.

In addition to the kinds of work mentioned above and a recent emphasis on the development of appropriate technology for different local situations around the world, there are more subtle aspects of daily life which can contribute to development or impede it. At the community level, the long-term commitment of the churches to the people of a particular place; to increase awareness of needs; to give opportunities for all to be part of the process and to share in the rewards of community efforts; to focus on the essential quality of life to preserve or achieve; to increase the confidence of those who first venture into change, these are immeasurable but basic social elements which must be nurtured.

CWS focuses on many aspects of development within the total

society. It pursues goals beyond merely increasing the gross national product (GNP) and per capita income. That could be achieved with large sectors of the population still left out, and with personal values ignored in the push for material advancement. The goal is development of total communities.

In development, churches are concerned for the quality of life of individuals. This is measured partly in numerical terms according to certain criteria that are of basic importance to the lives of the people. In 1973, United Nations Secretary General Kurt Waldheim called attention to a need for supplementing the GNP with other measurements of development. And a 1976 Club of Rome report called for a quality of life index. In response, the Overseas Development Council introduced its Physical Quality of Life Index (PQLI) in its publication *Agenda 77,* and that approach quickly gained widespread acceptance.

The PQLI for a country is obtained by averaging three statistics: infant mortality, life expectancy and literacy. The literacy figure is the actual percentage. For the other two, the worst performance anywhere in 1950 is taken as 0 and the best expected by the year 2000 is 100. This index serves to give a more reliable indication of development than financial indicators can measure.

For the churches, however, development also includes factors less susceptible to numerical measurement. These include the right of all people to participate in making the decisions that affect their lives. It includes a concern for justice. It includes full respect for the human rights of all people.

The churches turn first to the most needy, but do not leave out anybody. From a Christian perspective, they ask questions about life in affluent societies, including the American. What is the quality of life among people who enjoy an abundance of material goods? High income does not guarantee a high quality of life as enumerated in biblical terms. The quality of personal relationships among the people ranks higher.

Development assistance does focus on the poorer societies, however. And a key strategy in work for these societies in Asia, Africa and Latin America, commonly called the Third World, is regional planning. Human problems do not confine themselves to national boundaries. Problems such as those of the Sahel or southeast Asia are regional. The plan for the Africa emphasis of 1980-82 establishes four regional consultancies to assist colleague organizations, most of which are church-related, in all the countries of the respective regions.

Another principle of development is integrated planning to include all aspects of a society's needs. Food production may seem the most immediate requirement, but it may run parallel with a need for better understanding of nutrition. Programs of health care and preventative medicine are essential, including provisions for pure air and water. Education must be improved so people can develop the skills required to take command of community enterprise. All the components must work together.

Still another principle is introducing technology suitable to the developmental level a particular society has reached—appropriate technology. Usually it is not appropriate to ship American tractors to Third World countries. American-made equipment uses expensive fuel, requires trained operators and trained mechanics and stocks of spare parts. A $20,000 machine often sits idle in some remote area of the third world for lack of a $20 part.

As the world increasingly recognizes the necessity of developing economies that run on renewable resources and can sustain themselves through the end of the oil age and into a stable future. CWS development efforts have come to focus on sustainable technologies and self-generating projects.

The goals of development and human rights come together in emphasis on forms of development that will provide social justice, the right of all members of a society to participate in the decisions that govern their lives and respect for the rights of future generations.

CWS seeks to promote these principles not only through its own activities abroad but also through influencing the U.S. government's development policy. Since 1974, Larry Minear has worked in Washington as hunger consultant for CWS and Lutheran World Relief. He has worked with the President's World Hunger Working Group, the U.S. delegation to the United Nations 1978 World Food Council and the U.S. Agriculture Department's Task Force on PL 480 (Food for Peace).

As a link between the churches and government agencies, he also helps church agencies stay in touch with what is happening in the general field of development and advises them on aspects of government activity that could tie into church programs.

A special dimension of development is promoted by the Office of Family Life and Population Programs. Iluminado Rodriguez, director of the office, sees her work as an intrinsic element in development.

Not only must developing countries stabilize their population growth, she points out, but they must secure the contribution of women in development activity. Women cannot make their proper contribution, she says, if they must give all their energies to bearing and raising unlimited numbers of children.

When this office was established in 1965, it was called Family Planning. At that time, it concentrated on supplying contraceptives and educational materials about birth control.

But the churches came to believe that this approach was too narrow. So when Ms. Rodriguez took the post in 1975, succeeding another Filipino who had been her college teacher back in Manila, Epifania Resposo, she proposed a change to the present name.

Since 1965, governments in the developing countries have begun to do more of the basic work of providing contraceptives, so the need for churches to focus on that is not as great. But in any case, such a narrow approach brought problems.

For one thing, directed from the United States, it easily aroused suspicion and resentment. The perception of the program from the viewpoint of some Third World people was that comparatively rich Americans go into poor countries and tell people there to stop having so many children. They needed to show a broader concern for the welfare of a society. When advocates of family planning come with that perspective, then women in the developing countries of course want to limit the number of their children and space them, Ms. Rodriguez finds. So they gladly accept help.

CWS works through local groups. For example, in Bangladesh Ms. Rodriguez found a YWCA holding a sewing class for women. When she suggested that it include education in health and family planning, the director agreed but said the YWCA had no funds. So Ms. Rodriguez arranged for a $5000 grant. Later, when the International Planned Parenthood Foundation saw what was being achieved, it took over sponsorship. CWS did not withdraw, however, but started financing a similar program at another Bangladesh YWCA.

Ms. Rodriguez notes that the village programs sponsored by the Evangelical Church in Egypt include family education as an intrinsic part of development. "You can discern a visible difference in the villages that have had this program," she says. "There are fewer children, and the children they do have are better cared for and healthier."

But family education and planning lead on to the broader questions about women's place in society, Ms. Rodriguez points out. If they can plan their families and bear fewer children, then they have more time and energy for other things. So that presents the question of what they

Using appropriate materials and tools in agricultural development is crucial to long-term effectiveness. These men are making mud blocks for a storage building in a rural cooperative in Senegal.
(CWS photo/Hollon)

93

will do, and how society will make an enlarged place for them.

A mark of professional recognition for the Office of Family Life and Population Programs came in 1978 when it received its first grant from the United Nations Fund for Population Activities. The grant amounted to $9000 and went to an Integrated Maternal-Child Health Project in Recife, Brazil.

Bangladesh provides an example of the way churches work for development. After Indian troops secured the independence of Bangladesh in December 1971, representatives of church agencies in Norway, Sweden, Germany, England and the United States got together in Geneva and set up a Bangladesh Ecumenical Relief and Rehabilitation Service (BERRS), with an initial budget of $13 million.

An office was opened in Dacca, the capital, in early 1972. Giving the project an even broader international character, the coordinating committee placed there as director a native of Sri Lanka, Harris Amit. He had emigrated to Canada and was teaching at the Coady Institute, which trained students from developing countries for work in cooperatives. He was employed for one year to get the BERRS program underway.

The Bangladesh National Council of Churches then set up its own agency, the Christian Commission for Development in Bangladesh (CCDB), and, by agreement, took over the program in late 1972. Meanwhile, CWS had secured a $1 million contract from AID to build housing in Bangladesh, and that meant an American was needed to make the legal certification to AID that the money was properly used.

So CWS sent Howard Jost, a young Mennonite who had worked in the area as a volunteer when Bangladesh was still East Pakistan. He became assistant director, and when Mr. Amit's year was up, the Bangladesh churches had no one immediately available to head the CCDB, so Mr. Jost was made director.

A young Bangladeshi lawyer, Sushanta Adhikari, who had done relief and rehabiliation work after the 1970 cyclone, became associate director. And when Mr. Jost went for home leave in 1974, he took over the agency and Mr. Jost then returned to work under him from 1975 to 1977 as a consultant.

The churches' program in Bangladesh took several forms. Some food and clothing was distributed for emergency relief. Then for rehabilitation, the churches supported housing construction and replacement of some equipment that had been destroyed in the cyclone and then the war.

One need was replacement of barges and small ships that

transported grain and other products along the coast and up the many inland waterways. The churches were able to secure some used cargo coasters and self-propelled barges from Germany for this.

Later consequences of this gift illustrated a frequent experience of agencies assisting with development. Most any piece of machinery or equipment will require maintenance and repair. And when something breaks down, people of the developing country commonly expect the donor· agency to fix it.

Housing projects bring similar expectations. Giving people housing they cannot afford to repair will likely produce bitterness somewhere down the way. In some areas, people cannot afford to replace a window that gets broken. Who will do it then?

When the coasters and barges given to Bangladesh began to need spare parts, the operators turned to the CCDB. A similar sequence came with the gift of some two-way radios for communication between the Relief and Rehabilitation Ministry in Dacca and district towns. When they needed repair, Ministry officials came back to the churches for help.

In these cases, the CCDB was able to respond, but in some others it could not meet expectations. Churches have to recognize that whenever they make gifts, they will likely create demands for future contributions. This may seem unreasonable, but it is a natural human reaction. So churches working in development must plan ahead, ask whether the recipients of their gifts will be able to handle maintenance and work out clear agreements about who will take responsibility for upkeep.

Another part of the CCDB program was a rice project. Improved varieties were secured from the International Rice Research Institute (IRRI) in the Philippines. The intention was to put together a package including rice for planting, insecticides, hand-operated sprayers that would be manufactured in Bangladesh and an instruction booklet.

In the end, the CCDB found it could not get the sprayers made but that the country had others it could use. The instruction booklet included color pictures showing how the rice would look if certain insects attacked it, if it needed more fertilizer and so on. Farmers who had problems with their rice could look at these pictures and perhaps decide what was the cause in their fields.

At the beginning, BERRS also agreed to undertake a pilot health project for the government, and this later became a model for the country. It involved setting up a health system for one county, Company Thana, whose county seat was Company Ganj (town).

"Company" meant the British East India Company, which once operated a trading center there.

In the government health program, family planning was separate from other health services, and the pilot project sought to develop an integrated system. The government was never able to integrate its systems nationally as it had hoped, but other features of the pilot project became national models.

The model system included a hospital at the county seat and clinics in the villages. Nurses and paramedics would work in the clinics regularly, and doctors would visit from the hospital at certain times. Difficult cases would be sent to the hospital, either by the doctors during their visits or by the nurses and paramedics in emergency cases.

Another part of the project was training workers to deal with several aspects of health. The government health ministry already had men who visited every house regularly, but each one performed only one service, such as spraying for mosquitoes or checking on a particular disease. They were retrained so they could take a more comprehensive approach to family health.

Village women were recruited to work in family planning and to tie this work in with the clinics. At first, men of the area fiercely resisted the cultural innovation of letting women go about on their own from house to house. They vowed that their wives and daughters would never be allowed to do such a thing. But after a couple of women made the initial breakthrough, and began adding regular wages to the family income, the men began competing to get the jobs for women in their families.

In the cities, many women of better education were unemployed, and pressures came to use them for the family planning programs. But directors of the project decided in favor of recruiting village level women. These women were happy to get the salaries, even though they were small, and so did not take the jobs merely as a temporary stopgap until they could find something better. And unlike educated women of the cities, they liked working in the villages. So despite having less education, they were better suited. Giving jobs to women in the villages also helped hold families there rather than further encourage urban overcrowding.

As the government later set up training programs for the nurses who would operate clinics in other counties, it brought them to Company Thanh for field training.

Another part of the program was an evaluation that was conducted from the beginning, with financing from the Ford Foundation. As it became a model for use elsewhere, studies of its achievements and limitations were already available.

A South American example of CWS support for development is the Rural Development Project (RDP) operated by the Protestant churches of Chile through their agency, Diakonia. (This agency is separate from the similarly-named agency of the Brazilian Protestant churches, Diaconia.)

Through the RDP program, the churches have assisted some 1800 families who received small farms under land reform movements of the Salvador Allende government (1970-73) and its predecessor led by President Eduardo Frei.

Diakonia recognized that land reform, vital as it is to social justice in areas such as Latin America, does not in itself provide final answers to all problems. People who become small landholders for the first time need assistance of many kinds if they are to maintain their newly-secured economic status.

Usually they need credit to buy seed and other supplies, and even to help them pay living expenses from one crop to another. They also need advice from agricultural specialists because they are taking on levels of responsibility they usually have not known in the past.

Another need is for access to machinery they can't afford to buy but might rent for short periods. And they need help with marketing.

So unless someone helps with these needs, people confronting a host of unfamiliar challenges may prove unsuccessful, particularly in their first years. And since they will usually have no financial reserves, nor any well-to-do relatives who might tide them over a difficult period, they may be forced to sell their land in order to buy food.

The final result then is that the land gradually moves back into the hands of the rich, or of powerful corporations, and the old social structure reemerges.

Though Diakonia is an agency of Protestant churches, it hired a Catholic layman, Alejandro Aires, as coordinator of the project. He had training as an agronomist, which was the basic need for this project to help small farmers.

The project is concentrated in the central south regions of Nuble (Chillan) and Cautin (Temuco), areas where many people had received land and many were Protestant.

Mr. Aires, based in Santiago, and two assistants supervise ten agricultural specialists and ten home economists who work on the local level.

Also included in the project is a plan for training 100 peasant

A simple, yet effective, gravity feed irrigation system. Water is pulled from well by oxen.
(CWS photo/Hollon)

volunteers who will serve on development committees in "second level" organization. Diakonia stresses that development must be "human development," and not merely economic. Getting families together in ways that stimulate a sense of community solidarity is more important than merely increasing production.

But of course it does intend to help the farmers increase production. And it provides a variety of services, such as maintaining a rotating fund of capital to help finance purchase of farm supplies.

These aspects are necessary but from the church perspective not sufficient without certain other factors. "Dignity, self-respect and participation in the decisions that affect their lives are basic in order for people to have a clearer understanding of their rights and responsibilities, and for discovering themselves as children of God," says South America director Joel Gajardo.

Since Diakonia's Rural Development Project began under previous governments, he says, it got the assistance of government technicians. And the government of General Augusto Pinochet, who gained power in the military coup of 1973 in which President Allende was killed, did not find the particular activities of the project a threat. So it continued providing staff help.

"But doing business with a government opposed to the interest of the poor does not make sense," says Mr. Gajardo, a Chilean who was himself found objectionable by the Pinochet government and expelled. "So we encouraged them to break with it. But then they challenged us to increase our support to make up for the government help they would lose if they followed our suggestion."

As a consequence, the American churches, who had been contributing about $15,000 a year to Diakonia for this project, were encouraged to give $150,000 over a two-year period, starting in August 1979.

CWS has found its work intertwined with human rights at many points. Refugee and development work have inherent human rights implications since they give people the opportunity for survival and wider choice.

But CWS also makes specific contributions. It has made grants to the Vicariate of Solidarity established by the Catholic Church of Chile, with participation by some non-Catholics, to aid victims of the Pinochet government. It has aided black liberation groups in Africa. In Hong Kong, it supports the Society for Community Organization (SOCO), an agency that works for the rights of houseboat families. These families have been denied housing on land and forced to live on the water. They have been denied electricity, drinking water and even schools for their children.

In Indonesia, CWS has assisted the National Council of Churches in its program of support for political prisoners and their families.

Human rights issues have been particularly prominent in programs related to east Asia. In this area, where hunger and malnutrition pose less immediate threat than in some parts of Asia, churches can give proportionally more attention to human rights issues, reports area director Ed Luidens.

In these areas, which have enjoyed some degree of success in economic development, the churches are concerned about fair distribution of the gains. And this often brings them into conflict with the governments of the area.

Many church leaders of South Korea have been jailed because of their campaigns for fairer treatment of poor workers, rural and urban. The Korean Christian Academy in Seoul came under attack because of its program of training rural pastors and women church workers, called evangelistic women, to organize people or development. In 1979, a group of Academy staff members were tried and given three-to-seven year sentences upon conviction. They were accused of violations under the Anti-Communism Law.

Their legal defense was provided by a Legal Aid Fund of the Korean National Council of Churches. CWS has assisted both this fund and a committee set up by the Council to assist professors and students dismissed from other institutions for their human rights work.

The committee decided upon various research projects that would be useful in church or community work and gave the professors one-year assignments to pursue them. An economist might be assigned a project on church activity in development. Some of the professors were assigned to write histories relating to the upcoming 1984 centennial celebration of the first Protestant work in Korea.

Professors taking these assignments were given pay equal to one-third or one-half their former salaries, and this aid, limited though it was, enabled them to survive until they could make arrangements for some other kind of work. Some students, who had been living and in some cases supporting families on their scholarships and school-related jobs, were given temporary jobs as assistants to the professors.

The Korean Council of Churches has also set up an agency, the Korean Church Service Association, which serves as the CWS colleague agency on development. It runs such projects as a rice bank that lends seed rice to farmers and allows them to pay back, with a little rice interest, from their crops. In this way they are enabled to break their traditional dependence and sometimes virtual enslavement to usurious money lenders.

In Taiwan, another colleague agency, Taiwan Christian Service, has combined human rights and development emphases in its service to tribal people. In the past these people have lived by hunting, berry· picking and so on. But modern developments are pushing them out of their traditional mountain areas and into farming areas. They must adapt to an entirely different kind of life, so the churches teach them to begin planning food production cycles and planning their families, to clear land and to irrigate.

In recent years, CWS has become involved in human rights issues within the United States. Two examples are its support for people in the Love Canal area and for native Americans in the Southwest.

Both of these were groups that needed the enhanced strength that comes from having ties with a national organization. Corporations or government agencies find it easy to ignore protests and problems of ordinary people in a local area. But when some national body takes up their case and gives it national exposure, there is at least more attention paid, whether or not the final outcome is satisfactory.

In 1978 the Love Canal area of Niagara Falls, New York, was declared a health emergency area. The people there were living in homes built over a former dumping area for chemical wastes. A medical researcher found that more than half the babies born to families in that section of the city had birth defects, and that a fourth of the pregnancies resulted in miscarriages.

It became immediately obvious that the people had to find new homes and move. But the value of their homes in the Love Canal area immediately sank to zero. So they needed help from the corporations that had created the problem in the first place, and from the governments that had allowed it.

CWS helped the religious community of Niagara County and Western New York form an Ecumenical Task Force to help families caught in the disaster. It gave the Task Force a $3000 grant to take care of some of its initial expenses. And it arranged for a lawyer to serve six months as its legal counsel.

The case of the Indians involved a nuclear waste spillage on Navajo land at Church Rock, New Mexico. The Domestic Disaster Office of CWS joined with an ecumenical body of that area, the Inter-Church Agency of New Mexico, to offer aid.

Both of these projects also illustrate what many people see as a significant new trend of our era, the increasing frequency with which disasters come through human causation.

Working for development, CWS seeks not merely to support useful projects but to establish relationships that help local churches participate more effectively in the development of their countries.

When an agency delegation visited Cuba in September 1979, it worked out an agreement with the Ecumenical Council there and the Cuban government for support of a project in health care. This meant not only supplying medicines and medical equipment needed by the people of Cuba, it also resulted in an enchanced role for Cuban churches in the life of their nation. To strengthen the relationship still further, CWS arranged to bring European church agencies into the project. The CWS Committee later endorsed this project "as a means of manifesting the relationship it has with the churches of Cuba through the Ecumenical Council in Cuba."

At the end of 1979, CWS closed out a 20-year period of development work in Madagascar that began at the time the country became independent of French colonial rule. The work was taken over by an agency of the Madagascar churches, FRIKRIFA-MA (American Christian Help), which will continue to receive support.

It has been CWS policy to encourage formation of national church agencies that can take responsibility for work in their countries, and then channel resources from U.S. churches through them. In 1978 the Peru office turned over its program to a new agency formed by 12 churches, SEPAS (Social Action Service of Evangelical Churches in Peru). After Guatemala operations and the Madagascar work were both handed over to national agencies at the end of 1979, CWS carried on direct programs in only two countries, Haiti and Niger. And plans were underway for phasing out the Haiti program.

The increasing ability of national churches to take responsibility for programs to assist their people is central to the CWS concept of development.

In our world more people go to bed hungry each night than fed. Half of all humankind begin their working day unfortified. Their lives are a weary round of unrelieved poverty and deprivation. What they lack makes us all poorer, and every gain in health and hope in their lives enriches the life of all. When we involve ourselves to make the desert bloom, build roads to isolated communities, develop sources of water or electricity or skills, when we act as neighbors we become involved in the renewal of life. Those who are touched in this way see beyond the act of giving, they see the God of love who motivates the gift, who makes hope possible.

10

Into the Future

The world in which CWS will find itself working in the years ahead will be dominated by basic factors such as:

1. A move toward a new international economic, social and political order. In United Nations' forums, the developing countries that call themselves the Group of 77, the number of the original members though there are now more than 100, insist that justice requires a fundamental reordering of the world's economic system.

In this climate, CWS education of its own constituency will assume greater importance. The churches will call on it increasingly to educate American Christians to their global responsibility. It cannot just raise funds and operate apart from constituency understanding of its goals and methods.

Already the economic balance of the world has shifted considerably since CWS was founded in 1946. In its early years, the United States had wealth far greater than that of any other country, and American churches had material resources far beyond those available to churches elsewhere. So international aid was largely an American activity.

Today, Europe has recovered from World War II, and its churches now conduct their own aid programs. The German churches, through the tax support they receive, have much larger resources for aid than do the American churches. Nor do the Japanese churches stand in great need of material help, though they are numerically weak and now look for the support provided by psychological solidarity.

Other developments, such as OPEC's increases in oil prices, also serve to make the United States, and consequently its churches, proportionally less dominant in the world economy.

2. A move among mission churches around the world into autonomous status and new regional relationships among themselves.

Churches in the developing countries are gaining a surer sense of their own identity, and increased confidence in their ability to determine the direction of Christian witness among their people. They are correspondingly less inclined to look to Americans or Europeans for leadership.

What will be the role of American churches in this new situation? Do they have anything to offer besides dollars? What is the future role of American material aid? American personnel serving abroad?

American churches will need to realize that they can serve without engaging in a "mission expansion" program to enlarge their institutional presence abroad. They can adopt a supportive, cooperative stance that leaves them with plenty to do but free of activity that churches abroad consider imperialistic.

CWS does not think its role in the future will be merely reactive. The push of the developing countries for a new international order will affect the climate in which it works, but need not determine the decisions it makes about its role.

One service CWS can perform will be to think about alternative futures, and what can be done to help produce them for many of the world's impoverished peoples. How can the people of the Sahel move toward a future different from their past and present? What can the churches do that will assist the poor of Latin America in achieving a future according to their own design?

Another world issue facing CWS is the food crisis. In the last few years it has been alleviated to some extent. But in the 1980s it will be resolved in some more fundamental way, or it will become an immediate and acute crisis.

Recently the world has seen disruption in food production cycles in Iran, Kampuchea (Cambodia), parts of Africa and elsewhere. At the same time, greatly increased energy costs preclude the development of intensive Western-style agriculture in the poorer countries. And meanwhile population continues its rapid increases, putting more pressure on the limited food supplies of the present.

With active assistance by government and private groups working in development, food production might be increased by greater use of appropriate technology and through putting into production some land that is still unused. But the 1980s will be crucial for developmental activities and for attainment of a quality of life.

During the life span of CWS the mood of the American churches has gone through three phases:

1. They entered the period following World War II with a sense of triumphalism. The churches were crowded. A lot of money was coming in, and a lot of missionaries were going out. The American churches felt they were writing heroic new chapters of the Book of Acts.

2. That period ended as the 1950s came to a close. Then came the period of dealing with new forces of black power, liberation theology and other themes related to Exodus, coming out of bondage. The churches attempted to identify with these forces.

3. In the present period, the church around the world is becoming the church under duress. The theme of the 1980s will be that of the Book of Revelation—faithfulness. In many places the church has its back to the wall. In Sri Lanka it has lost much of its top leadership. In Cuba, the Protestant churches have declined from 300,000 at the time of the Revolution to 80,000 now. And they lost 75 per cent of their clergy.

This third phase has grown in part out of the second, as the shadow side of some positive developments. In the period of Exodus, many mission churches became independent and asserted their separate identity more forcefully. But this meant they were no longer closely identified as part of a strong international body, so they became more vulnerable to other forces. The impact of secularism, nationalism and other religions began to hit them harder because they were trying to stand in greater independence from their mother churches.

But many of the mission sending churches in the United States and Europe are themselves getting hit by these forces now. In the past, American churches have written papers on the theology of giving; in the future they may need to write more on the theology of receiving.

As CWS looks to the 1980s and beyond, it faces two types of questions: those relating to the direction of world forces and those growing out of its own internal structure.

Among the latter are questions about the type of personnel employed. In the years ahead, CWS will need to move toward more internationalizing of its personnel. When a staff member is needed for a new program in a Third World country, it might look to churches in other Third World countries, rather than employ another American.

Another issue CWS and its member churches will need to face in the 1980s is the dichotomy of mission and service. Is it valid to separate these two aspects of church activity at all? How valid is the structural separation that has been built into the denominations and ecumenical agencies? Within the National Council of Churches, the Division of Overseas Ministries has sought to bring mission and service into a closer relationship, but many people think the integration should now go further.

On the other hand, if mission and service become totally identified, could the churches perhaps lose something of the sense of breadth in their responsibility? Uniting the two entirely might turn out to mean that everything became service and the churches would lose any distinctive sense of proclaiming a Christian gospel. Or it might turn out to mean that everything became mission and the churches would lose the sense of a foot-washing ministry to the neediest of the world's people.

Some people are raising the question of whether relief and development aid constitute a pacifying force that helps keep oppressed people from rising up to demand fundamental change. This issue will likely become more acute in the future, and the churches will have to address it.

When a disaster situation in some country has dramatized the inadequacy of the government in helping its people, should foreign relief agencies rush in to get the government off the hook by alleviating the worst of the suffering? Or should they hold back some and allow the people to see that their basic need is not temporary aid from outside but new structures for handling their own problems? But if people are suffering now, can churches refuse to help on the theory that political change sometimes in the future might bring them a better life?

If CWS concludes that even its long range rehabilitation and development programs represent only a band aid approach to situations that require major surgery, how far can it go in stimulating change? If it rejects the idea of interfering in the political life of other countries, does that leave it without any role?

As mission churches in the developing countries have become independent, they have sometimes developed a ghetto mentality and tended to draw into a shell, rather than reaching out to serve their societies. Usually they have also been left with an institutional structure created by outsiders, rather than one growing out of their own situation, and they may spend a disproportionate amount of their energies just trying to keep the institution going.

What is the CWS role in such a situation? Can it find a way to continue strenghtening the national church, still respect that church's integrity and judgment, and yet encourage it to undertake a broader ministry?

CWS is committed to working through churches wherever they exist. But it cannot get involved in supporting their institutional structures. So if they are not ready to undertake programs of service to their societies, it will simply wait with patience until they are ready.

CWS will not try to go around the churches and conduct its own program apart from them. In the few cases where it tried something like that in the past, it failed. Christians cannot accept any basic separation of service from preaching and worship. All elements of Christian witness must be held together.

Through the 1980s, the churches will need to continue wrestling with the question of what Christian service means. In what way does it differ from any other kind of service?

Should the churches just assume they know what Christian service is, and that the only question is doing more of what they have been doing? How do the churches distinguish their service role from that of government, political parties and other agencies when they often appear on the surface to be doing much of the same kind of work?

How will American churches respond when their offers of service are rejected in other countries? In the past they have had to face the reality that some countries were no longer willing to admit their missionaries. In the future, their service efforts may sometimes encounter the same rejection.

India, which has long viewed missionaries askance, has decided that it no longer wants Americans to ship it their used clothing. The government of India has made this feeling inescapably plain by refusing to allow gifts of used clothing to enter the country duty free. And as a matter of policy, CWS never ships material aid to a country when duty is imposed.

India's action was apparently a matter of concern for national dignity, the government concluding that gifts of second hand clothes from a foreign country were demeaning. It may also have felt such gifts discouraged the growth of the clothing industry within India. When people could no longer get free clothing from abroad, they presumably would realize they had to produce their own.

On such questions, CWS will doubtless continue to find great variation among governments. But it will have to be asking whether its service programs serve to build dignity and self-reliance among those it intends to help, or whether they perhaps contribute more to an American sense of superiority.

An internal question for CWS concerns its relationships with sectors of American Christianity that are not currently part of its constituency. If its goal is to serve as an ecumenical vehicle for the American churches, should it work to make its ecumenical scope wider than at present? What should be its future relationships to U. S. Catholics, Southern Baptists and such groups as the evangelicals?

The mainline denominations that provide the core of CWS support have suffered some declines in membership and national program over the past 10-15 years. What does this mean for the future of CWS?

Member denominations give it less than it raises through CROP and less than it receives from government. What do the member denominations think about their responsibility to an agency that ostensibly operates as their agency? Do they want to see it become increasingly an agency of the government and other supporters?

National Council of Churches guidelines say its units should "normally" depend on church contributions for their programs and seek governing board approval before accepting government grants. But this approval is given rather routinely. Are the churches facing up to their financial responsibility for agencies they have created to carry out their programs?

The overall CWS relationship with government will remain a continuing issue. To what degree should a church agency cooperate with government programs? In the past CWS distributed far more Food for Peace commodities than at present. But it came to see that this program was largely directed to serving American foreign policy interests rather than merely serving the needs of the hungry.

In 1974, when the United States was vainly trying to save the anti-communist Lon Nol government of Kampuchea, it gave five times as much food to that country as to Bangladesh with its population ten times as large. Similar political orientations have been evident in Point Four, Alliance for Progress and other government programs.

CWS began scaling down its distribution of Food for Peace commodities in the 1960s. In dollar value, they constituted 85 per cent of its Material Resources Program in 1957, but dropped to 19 per cent by 1975. They later rose slightly, but in 1978 were only 22 per cent—$3.6 million out of a $16 million total.

In pounds, the decline went from 359.1 million in 1957 to 22.2 million in 1975 and 31.5 million in 1978. In pounds, Food for Peace still constituted nearly half of all shipments—31.5 million out of 65.9 million. The rest consisted of clothing, bedding and textiles (3 million), health and medical supplies (1 million), agricultural self-help

(200,000), food (30 million) and miscellaneous (200,000).

By 1979, CWS distributed Food for Peace commodities in only five countries—Haiti, Dominican Republic, Peru, India and Indonesia. That was a decline from 14 countries a decade earlier.

CWS has also received a number of large disaster and development grants from AID. To what extent should it get involved in administering large projects such as these grants serve to finance? If the churches decide they cannot provide adequate funds for CWS to do the work it thinks ought to be done, should they encourage it to look increasingly to government and other sources? In what ways is the character of an agency affected by the direction it turns in seeking funds?

On the other hand, CWS does not favor any absolute separation between church or other voluntary agencies and government. The American churches are a part of American society, and validly participate in activities of their society. When these activities are expressed through government programs that the churches are able to approve, then they need not stand aloof just because the programs are organized through the government. An excessive preoccupation with avoiding any touch of government, lest they be contaminated, could easily lead the churches into self-righteousness. And CWS certainly would oppose any effort undertaken from the side of government to exclude churches and other voluntary agencies from participation in national programs.

Refugee service and resettlement is another area that will need some reexamination in the years ahead. Nothing visible today suggests that the number of crisis situations creating refugees will decrease, or the tensions that keep refugees from returning to their homes. CWS has worked with Palestinian refugees for more than 30 years now. The Indochina refugees going into camps in Thailand and other Asian countries could remain equally long. They cannot all be resettled in the West, and it seems unlikely that they could return to their homelands in the foreseeable future. How will the churches develop a realistic program to serve their needs?

CWS must also reexamine refugee resettlement in the United States, says director Paul McCleary. Many of the refugees coming here from Cuba and Vietnam were middle class people who immigrated because they did not want to live under a socialist economic system. Their expectation and the expectation of American churches helping them resettle is that they will become middle class Americans. How realistic is that? And what will be the long term psychological costs to

110

the refugees?

Many of the Cuban refugees continue to orient their lives in relation to Cuba, and they maintain immigrant societies that disagree so strongly with each other that they are continually resorting to violence. The level of violence in American society has been increased by importing these conflicts.

Churches must give closer attention to what governments are doing in relation to some of these refugee situations. When the U.S. government sponsored "freedom flights" to bring out large numbers of Cuban refugees, it apparently wished to weaken Cuba by drawing out much of the educated professional and business leadership. On the other hand, the Cuban government was suspected of wanting to get rid of dissident citizens who might prove troublesome to it.

When governments are serving their own varied political interests in such situations, at the expense of individuals involved, the role of a Christian service agency requires careful thought lest it naively allow itself to be used for less than Christian purposes. This does not mean the churches will become any less willing to help people in need, but that they will exercise wisdom in the way they relate themselves to the world's many questionable political forces.

Conclusion

In August 1975 in the course of a week in Philadelphia over 900,000 Roman Catholics gathered to celebrate a Eucharistic Congress. The theme of the Congress was the Hungers of Mankind. Distinguished church leaders spoke on the great dangers to the world with millions of people suffering from physical hunger. Others spoke on spiritual hunger, the longing of the human spirit for forgiveness and salvation. Another address was on the hunger for identity. Three of the speakers spoke on the universal hunger for peace, the hunger for justice and economic development. These are concerns we all could identify with, the concern about the kind of world people are living in, the quality of life, the kind of world their children will inherit.

The outcome of the war on hunger by the year 2000 and beyond will be determined not by forces beyond human control, but by decisions well within the capability of nations and people working individually and together. To this end Church World Service will dedicate itself as part of God's answer. I have often thought of the story of the Good Samaritan as I have travelled across the world. This story will not be recreated in us by an extra effort to give a little more for the sake of the poor man by the side of the Jericho Road. We must somehow find a way to take his hand, heal his wounds, and get him to the Inn and provide for him in such a way that there will be manifested we are servants of him who wills a radical transformation of the life of the world.

Church World Service lives in a world of rapid social change but its ministry to human need remains unchanged. The methods will vary, yet the motivation for our response remains constant. "The love of

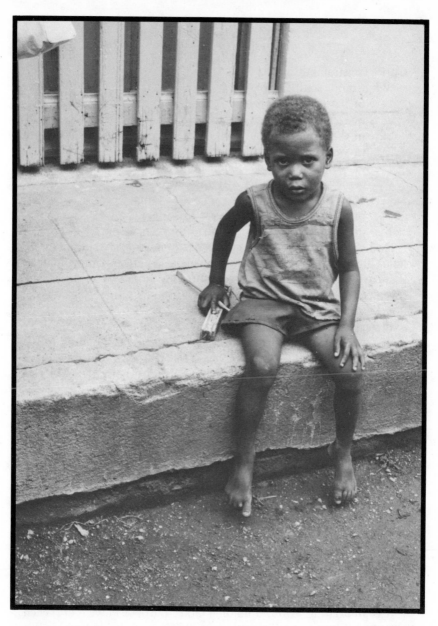

Dominican child sits in bewilderment after being separated from his family during Hurricane David in 1979. CWS's colleague agency Servicio Social de Iglesias Dominicanas provided emergency relief and coordinated long-term development aid in the Dominican Republic.

(CWS photo/Hollon)

Christ constraineth us."

What more shall I say
... of the hungry who have been fed
... of refugees who have been resettled
... of the wounded who have been lifted up and healed
... of wells that have been drilled
... of women who have found hope in family planning clinics
... of new crops that have flourished
... of new hope
... of loving concerns expressed in so many ways
... of quiet, anonymous ministries of compassion?

And so, we have come full circle. We do not know what the future holds but we do know God is in control of the future. Unfortunately, there will continue to be human suffering borne of injustice and revealed in poverty, hunger, disease and the wanderings of the homeless.

In the past decade and a half which we have covered in this book we have seen that the church is not only capable of responding to the hungers of the world, but that it is anxious to do so. Moreover, we have seen that the church has "staying power" which helps develop long term responses to injustice.

In these pages we have explored those responses in nearly every part of the world. Yet, of the terrifying events we have seen, we have not been merely unwilling witnesses. From Kampuchea to the Dominican Republic, from Uganda to Hong Kong, from Love Canal to Pakistan we have been joined together with our brothers and sisters on this small planet in a network of partnership which reaches out to people and says in the name of God: "We care about you."

We stand in solidarity with those who search for justice. We join with those who seek a home. We stand not only in spirit but also in deed, recognizing that to do so is often risky, sometimes frightening and always challenging.

We learn as much as we teach. We receive as much as we give. We are changed as much as we seek to create change.

It is an exciting world, unfolding God's purpose in each era, each new day. For we who live under the claim of Christian faith, it is a world of the cross—death and resurrection; of the basin and the towel—the servanthood of the Church. With these symbols of a vital, dynamic faith we approach the uncertain future in humility but with hope.

We will face difficult and imperfect choices but together with our brothers and sisters we will make them. If we do not know the shape of things to come with exactness, we do know that the human family will face terrifying events and frightening changes. And we also know that with the people of God who in partnership in Church World Service act in our behalf and in cooperation with brothers and sisters in colleague agencies in every part of the world, we will face whatever comes with hope and resolve, for another lesson we have learned is that when we care for each other and express our concern, it makes a difference. And that is what we want Church World Service to do—to make a difference in the world for "the love of Christ constraineth us."

> Then the righteous will answer him,
> "Lord, when did we see thee hungry and feed thee,
> or thirsty and give thee drink? And
> when did we see thee a stranger and welcome thee,
> or naked and clothe thee? And when did we
> see thee sick or in prison and visit thee?"
> And the King will answer them,
> "Truly, I say to you, as you did it to one of
> the least of these my brethren, you did it to me."
> (Matthew 25:37, 40 RSV)

CWS Material Resources Program 1946-1979

Material shipped	Pounds	Value
Clothing, Blankets	193,140,137	$122,236,137
Health, Medical (medicines, bandages, hospital equipment)	64,786,492	89,437,798
Agriculture Self-help (tractors, windmills, farm tools)	33,742,103	7,676,771
Food for Peace (Public Law 480 surplus commodities available through the U. S. government)	4,238,537,695	314,201,691
CROP Food (Commodities such as beans or rice purchased with funds raised through the Community Hunger Appeal of Church World Service)	116,993,511	17,092,441
Self-help (Office supplies, school kits for children, vehicles for distributing commodities)	43,919,374	14,130,376
Grand Totals	4,691,119,312	$564,775,214

The World

The world's homeless

(Refugees not permanently settled, mostly in camps)

Countries of asylum are in **bold face** type. regions or countries of origin are in light face type

Source: Office of U.S. Coordinator for Refugee Affairs

Italy—10,000
Soviet Union

Greece—5,000
Lebanon and Iraq

Cyprus—200,000
Internally displaced

Gaza Strip—354,000
Palestinians

Syria—198,000
Palestinians

Iran—35,000
Iraq

Afghanistan—100,000
Pakistan

Jordan—683,000
Palestinians

West Bank of Jordan River—310,000
Palestinians

Philippines—4,000
Indochina

Taiwan—1,000
Indochina

Hong Kong—44,000
Indochina

Vietnam—400,000
Cambodia

Indonesia—30,000
Indochina

Singapore—1,000
Indochina

Malaysia—75,000
Indochina

Thailand—161,000
Cambodia, not including 100,000 Khmer Rouge followers

Bangladesh—370,000
Burma 120,000; Biharis 250,000

Lebanon—212,000
Palestinians

Honduras—16,300
Nicaragua

Costa Rica—2,500
Nicaragua

Algeria—25,000
former Spanish Sahara

Djibouti—25,000
Ethiopia and Somalia

Sudan—256,000
Ethiopia 250,000; Zaire 3,500; Uganda 3,000

Cameroon—30,000 to 35,000
Equatorial Guinea

Gabon—60,000 to 70,000
Equatorial Guinea

Zaire—136,000
Angola 125,000; Burundi 11,000

Angola—20,000 to 30,000
South-West Africa

South-West Africa—4,000
Angola

Botswana—20,000
Zimbabwe Rhodesia

Zambia—55,200
Zimbabwe Rhodesia 40,000; Angola 23,000; South-West Africa 2,200

Zimbabwe Rhodesia—500,000
Internally displaced

Mozambique—70,000
Zimbabwe Rhodesia

Tanzania—161,500
Burundi 134,000; Rwanda 24,000; Uganda 3,500

Kenya—6,000
Uganda

Somalia—200,000
Ethiopia

Ethiopia—608,000
Sudan 8,000; internally displaced 600,000

Participating Denominations and Related Organizations

African Methodist Episcopal Church
African Methodist Episcopal Zion Church
American Baptist Churches, U.S.A.
The American Lutheran Church
Antiochian Orthodox Christian Archdiocese of N. America
Christian Church (Disciples of Christ)
Church of the Brethren
Church of God
Churches of God in North America
Community Churches
Cumberland Presbyterian Church
The Episcopal Church
Evangelical Covenant Church of America
Friends United Meeting
Greek Orthodox Archdiocese of North and South America
Heifer Project, Inc.
Hungarian Reformed Church in America
Lutheran Church in America
Lutheran Church—Missouri Synod
Mennonite Central Committee
Moravian Church in America
National Baptist Convention of America
National Council of Community Churches
Presbyterian Church in the U.S.
Reformed Church in America
Russian Orthodox Church in America
Serbian Eastern Orthodox Church
Seventh-day Adventists
Seventh Day Baptists
United Church of Christ
The United Methodist Church
The United Presbyterian Church in the U.S.A.